Islam

Originally Published by
Argus Communications
A Division of DLM, nc.
Niles, Illinois 60648 U.S.A.

Islam

BY ISMA'IL R. AL FARUQI, Ph.D.

PHOTO CREDITS

Bruno Barbey/MAGNUM PHOTOS, INC. 38
Eileen Darby/FREE LANCE PHOTOGRAPHERS GUILD 79
Edwards/FREE LANCE PHOTOGRAPHERS GUILD 43
R. Manley/SHOSTAL ASSOCIATES cover: bottom left
Douglas Pike/BRUCE COLEMAN INC. 66
Marc Riboud/MAGNUM PHOTOS, INC. 55
P. Schmid/SHOSTAL ASSOCIATES cover: top right
SHOSTAL ASSOCIATES 6, 22
Mateen Siddiqui 15, 31, 63, 71
Bernard G. Silberstein/FREE LANCE PHOTOGRAPHERS GUILD 47
Sipa Press/EDITORIAL PHOTOCOLOR ARCHIVES cover: top left, bottom right
Lee Trail/DON ARTHUR TORGERSEN PRODUCTIONS cover: middle right
D. Warren/SHOSTAL ASSOCIATES 26

MAP AND COVER DESIGN

Gene Tarpey

Printed in the United States of America.

International Graphics
4411 41st Street
Brentwood, Maryland 20722
Telephone: (301) 779-7774

International Standard Book Number: 0-89505-022-6

Library of Congress Number: 79-84209

0 9 8 7 6 5 4 3

Contents

Foreword

"The study of religion is the study of mankind." Religion touches the deepest feelings of the human heart and is part of every human society. In modern times religion has been studied by sociologists and anthropologists as a cultural institution. Psychologists see religion as an expression of an inner human need. Philosophers view it as a system of thought or doctrine. Historians consider religion a part of the intellectual and institutional development of a given era.

What is religion? Modern definitions range from "what man does in his solitude" to "an expression of collective identity," and from "man's experience of awe and fascination before a tremendous mystery" to "projective feelings of dependency." The scope of life that religion is identified with is so vast, and the assumptions about the nature of religion are so varied, that we may readily agree with those who say that the study of religion is the study of mankind.

Religion takes many forms, or perhaps it would be better to say that there are many aspects to religion. They include *belief* (e.g., the belief in a creator God), *ritual action* (e.g., making offerings to that God), *ethical action* (following God's law), the formation of *religious communities,* and the formulation of *creeds and doctrinal systems.*

Joachim Wach, a scholar of religion, has pictured religion in terms of religious experience which expresses itself in thought, action, and fellowship.[1] In this view religion is rooted in religious experience, and all other aspects of religion are expressions of that experience. For example, the Buddha's experience of the highest Truth (in Buddhism called *Nirvana*) led him to teach what he had experienced (known as *dharma*) and resulted in the formation of a monastic community (known as *sangha*).

It must be remembered that religions develop within particular historical and cultural traditions and not in a vacuum. This fact has several profound consequences for the study of religion. In the first place it means that religion can never be completely separated from particular historical and cultural traditions. For example, early Christian thought was deeply influenced by both Semitic and Greek traditions, and such central Christian celebrations as Christmas and Easter owe their form to pre-Christian European traditions.

---

[1]Joachim Wach, *The Comparative Study of Religions* (New York: Columbia University Press, 1958).

Furthermore, since a religion is subject to cultural and historical influences, its traditions are always developing relative to particular times and places. For example, the form of worship used in the Buddhist Churches of America (founded in the late nineteenth century) has as much or more in common with American Protestant worship services than with its traditional Japanese form. A religion, then, as part of a specific historical and cultural stream, changes through time and can be fully understood only in relationship to its historical and cultural forms. By way of generalization we might say that Christianity as a religion is only partially understood in terms of its central beliefs and that a fuller or more complete understanding demands a knowledge of its worldwide history and the influence of its various cultural traditions.

In the second place, since a religion develops within particular historical and cultural settings, it also influences its setting. In other words, there is a give-and-take relationship between a religion and its environment. For example, in traditional societies like medieval Europe, Christianity was the inspiration for much of the art and architecture. The same is true for traditional India, where Buddhism and Hinduism decisively affected artistic forms, or for traditional Persia with Islam. Of course, religion influences its environment in other than merely artistic realms. It has had profound effects on modes of behavior (ethics), conceptions of state (politics), forms of economic endeavor—indeed, on all aspects of life.

As a consequence of the pervasive influence of religion in so many aspects of human endeavor, students of religion and society have observed that in traditional societies religion was never isolated. That is, nothing within the given society was perceived as nonreligious or profane. Every meaningful act was seen as religious or sacred. Professor Robert Bellah of the University of California at Berkeley argues that in the West the split between the sacred and the profane or the differentiation of religion from other aspects of life did not really begin until about the time of the Protestant Reformation. He refers to that period as "early modern." Beginning with the early modern period onward to the present, religion has become more and more differentiated from Western culture. Thus, for example, it is no longer assumed that an American is a Protestant, whereas it is still largely assumed that a Thai is a Buddhist.

The question has been asked, "Can someone understand a religion in which he or she does not believe?" As the previous discussion of the nature of religion indicates, belief in the truth claims of a religious tradition is not a prerequisite for engaging in its study or even for understanding (i.e., making sense of) its beliefs and historical forms. The study of religion, however, does demand empathy and sympathy. To engage in the study of another religion for the purpose of proving that one's own is superior can only result in a distorted understanding of that tradition. Or, for that matter, if one who professes no religious belief approaches the study of religion with an inhibiting skepticism, then the beauty and richness of religion will be lost. For the believer, the study of another religious tradition should enhance his or her own faith-understanding; for the nonbeliever (i.e., agnostic), the study of religion should open up new dimensions of the human spirit.

The objective study of religion should be undertaken because of its inherent significance—because the understanding of cultures and societies, indeed, of humankind, is severely limited when such study is ignored. The study of our own tradition from its own particular creedal or denominational perspective is justifiably a part of our profession of faith. However, such study should not close us off from a sympathetic understanding of other religious traditions. Rather, such inquiry should open us to what we share in common with other religious persons, as well as to what is genuinely unique about our own religious beliefs and traditions.

Is the study of religion relevant today? The authors of this series believe the answer is a resounding "Yes!" The United States—indeed, the world—is in the midst of a profound transition period. The crisis confronting nations today cannot be reduced merely to economic inflation, political instability, and social upheaval. It is also one of values and convictions. The time has passed when we can ignore our crying need to reexamine such basic questions as who we are and where we are going—as individuals, as communities, and as a nation. The interest in Islam on the part of many American blacks, experimentation with various forms of Asian religions by the "Age of Aquarius" generation, and a resurgence of Christian piety on college campuses are particular responses to the crisis of identity through which we are currently passing.

The serious study of religion in the world today is not only legitimate but necessary. Today we need all of the forces we can muster in order to restore a sense of individual worth, moral community, and value direction. The sympathetic study of religion can contribute toward these goals and can be of assistance in helping us to recover an awareness of our common humanity too long overshadowed by our preoccupation with technological and material achievement. As has been popularly said, we have conquered outer space at the expense of inner space.

But why study non-Western religions? The reason is quite simple. We no longer live in relative isolation from the cultures of Asia and Africa. As a consequence the marketplace of ideas, values, and faiths is much broader than it used to be. We are in contact with them through popular books and the news media, but for the most part our acquaintance is superficial at best. Rather than looking at the religions imbedded in these cultures as quaint or bizarre—an unproductive enterprise—we should seek genuine understanding of them in the expectation of broadening, deepening, and hopefully clarifying our own personal identity and direction. The study of religion is, then, a twofold enterprise: engaging the religion(s) as it is, and engaging ourselves in the light of that religion.

The Argus Communications Major World Religions Series attempts to present the religious traditions of Judaism, Christianity, Islam, Hinduism, Buddhism, China, and Africa in their unity and variety. On the one hand, the authors interpret the traditions about which they are writing as a faith or a world view which instills the lives of their adherents with value, meaning, and direction. On the other hand, each volume attempts to analyze a particular religion in terms of its historical and cultural settings. This latter dimension means that the authors are interested in the present form of a religious tradition as well as its past development. How can Christianity or Judaism speak to the problems confronting Americans today? What are some of the new religions of Africa, and are they displacing traditional beliefs and world views? Can Maoism be considered the new religion of China? Is traditional Hinduism able to cope with India's social, economic, and political change? The answers to such questions form a legitimate and important part of the content of the series.

The author of each volume is a serious student and teacher of the tradition about which he or she is writing. Each has spent considerable time in countries where that religious tradition is part of the culture. Furthermore, as individuals, the authors are committed to the positive value the proper study of religion can have for students in these times of rapid social, political, and economic change. We hope that the series succeeds in its attempt to present the world's religions not as something "out there," a curiosity piece of times past, but as a subject of study relevant to the needs of our times.

Preface

Islam is the most misunderstood of the world religions. The reasons for this are many and varied. Primary among them is Islam's long confrontation with Christianity.

When Islam arose in the seventh century C.E.,[1] it spread across continents with shocking speed. Its political power eventually eclipsed that of the Roman Empire—the greatest political and social organization the world had ever known.

The convincing logic of Islam's theological claim, the ennobling uplift of its pietism and morality, the pragmatic efficiency of its law, the appeal of its universality, and the moving commitment and liberality of its adherents—all these disarmed the millions and persuaded them to join its ranks. For a thousand years Islam was unparalleled in its world power, affluence, high civilization, and culture. For a thousand years it was the only challenger of Europe, and it came close to making a conquest of that continent. Europe sent a dozen crusades against Islam to no avail. Another campaign launched by Christendom in Spain succeeded and brought to an end seven centuries of Islamic domination in the Iberian Peninsula. But it was only in the last two centuries that Europe succeeded in conquering the Muslim World and subjecting it to colonial fragmentation and rule. Even so, the religion of Islam continued to spread in Asia and Africa at a greater pace than did Christianity, despite the support Christian missionaries received from the colonial powers.

This long history of confrontation and conflict gave rise to countless rumors and fabrications designed to place Islam and its adherents in a bad light. Together with misunderstandings of the Islamic religion and culture, the antagonistic allegations became built-in prejudices, hard to shake off. Therefore, the student of Islam needs to take special care to approach the subject with an open and sympathetic mind.

---

[1]C.E. stands for "Common Era" and is widely used instead of A.D., which is specifically Christian in reference.

The rewards of such care are great. Genuine understanding of Islam will reveal to the student that Islam, the religion, is a later moment of that very consciousness which produced Judaism and Christianity; and that Islam, the culture, is as much a source of Western civilization as classical Greece and Rome. Once Islam is understood, it becomes easy for one to relate to its adherents in understanding and fellowship. That is what the reader is here invited to do.

Isma'il R. al Faruqi
Temple University
Philadelphia, Pennsylvania

Chapter 1

The Phenomenon of Islam

The religious movement that began in Arabia in the seventh century C.E. has spread around the globe, becoming one of the world's major religions. Just how did this movement begin? Where is Islam practiced today? What is the current Muslim population? What does it mean to be a Muslim? These and other questions relating to the phenomenon of Islam are answered in this chapter.

WHO IS A MUSLIM?

The number of Muslims in the world today is a subject of controversy. Unfortunately, the controversy cannot be solved at present. In some countries a census has not been taken for many years. Some governments are interested in belittling or exaggerating the number of their Muslim citizens. In still other countries, such as the U.S.S.R. and China, no census may distinguish the Muslims from their non-Muslim compatriots. No account of the numbers of Muslims is hence absolutely trustworthy. The *United Nations Statistical Yearbook* relies on the figures supplied by governments. Its figures are subject to the "official" viewpoint taken by governments—whether they are non-Muslim, secular, or antireligious and hence prone to underestimate, or whether they are Muslim and hence prone to overestimate. According to the U.N., the world Muslim population is 538 million;[1] according to Muslim governments, one billion.[2] Even if we take the lesser figure, the Muslims constitute a significant portion of the world's population of four billion. At least one out of every seven persons in the world is a Muslim.

Muslims constitute the majorities of many countries and significant minorities in other countries. The map of the Muslim World looks like a solid rectangle running over the great landmass of Africa-Asia. It

---

[1]*United Nations Statistical Yearbook* (1975); *United Nations Statistical Review* (1973); *Encyclopaedia Britannica Book of the Year* (1976).
[2]Muslim World League, Makkah and New York.

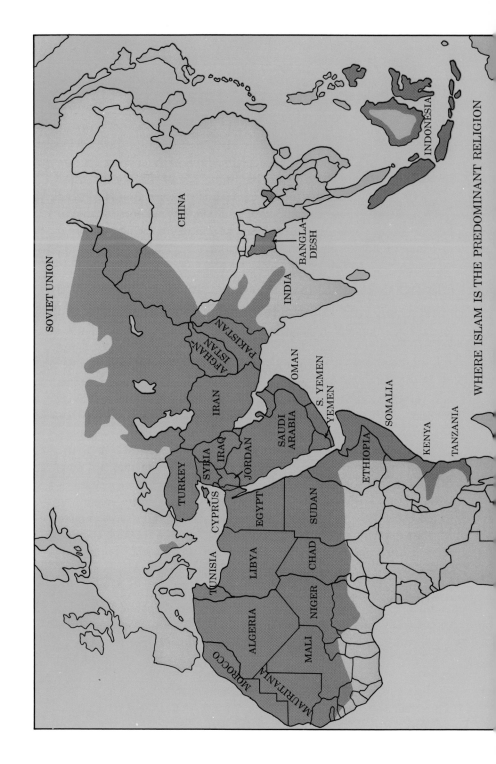

WHERE ISLAM IS THE PREDOMINANT RELIGION

stretches from Dakar, the westernmost corner of Africa, all the way to Sinkiang in northwest China. The rectangle seems to have three long fingers: one stretching over the east coast of Africa, a second along the great river plains of northern India and reaching to the Bay of Bengal, and a third stretching over the entire archipelago of the East Indies and including the Philippines, New Guinea, and Java. By continents, Muslims are divided as follows: 8,370,000 live in Europe;[3] 430,267,000 in Asia, including the Middle East;[4] and about 90,000,000 in Africa.[5]

There are no accurate figures for Muslims in North America. About half of the North American Muslims are members of the World Community of Islam in the West (formerly called Bilalians, or Black Muslims). The other half are black and white Americans and Canadians, as well as immigrants and their descendants. Most North American Muslims live in the large cities. Many American towns have mosques, or houses of prayer, where Muslims worship. The largest and most beautiful of these is the mosque in Washington, D.C., completed in the 1960s under the patronage of a number of Muslim governments.

All Muslims know some measure of Arabic since Arabic is the language of worship. Many have achieved varying degrees of mastery of the language since it is the first language of Islamic religious thought and culture. Persons speaking and writing nothing but Arabic could find themselves at home anywhere in the worldwide belt of Muslim communities.

Arabic calligraphy (elegant handwriting) and arabesque decoration are prominent and visible everywhere Muslims congregate. This is especially true in the houses of worship, or mosques, where verses from the Qur'an (Koran), written in beautiful calligraphy, decorate the walls. Equally universal are certain architectural features of those buildings, such as the minarets (towers) from which the muezzin chants the call to worship in Arabic five times a day. The call to prayer, as well as the chanting of the Qur'an, is heard throughout the Muslim World. There are, of course, other features which bind the Muslim

---

[3]*Encyclopaedia Britannica Book of the Year* (1976).
[4]Ibid.
[5]*United Nations Statistical Review* (1973).

*The shaded portions of this map indicate
those areas where Islam is the predominant religion
in Africa and Asia.*

World together, but they are less conspicuous. They reveal themselves to the investigator, if not to the casual tourist.

Muslims have great diversity in appearance. They are divided into many cultural groups, each carrying its own dress, customs, and ways of life. In the past, the Muslim World has witnessed a great deal of mobility among its peoples. The brotherhood, racial tolerance, and lack of color discrimination—the common institutions of the Muslims—once made it possible for anyone to move from one end of the empire to another without estrangement. As a direct effect of this mobility, Muslim urban populations are very mixed. This is more than evident to anyone sitting at a sidewalk cafe in Rabat, Tripoli, Cairo, Damascus, Jiddah, Baghdad, Teheran, Lahore, Delhi, or Jakarta. Passing by are automobiles as well as camels; veiled women as well as women in saris and miniskirts, jeans and sarongs; fair and blue-eyed northerners as well as blacks, West African Hamites, Chinese, or Mongols; small-built Malays or large-bodied Afghans; men with parted hair and men with fezzes and turbans; men in Western clothing and men in flowing robes. All of them are Muslims.

The same diversity is beginning to characterize the Muslim presence in North America. Whereas half of the Muslims of this continent are blacks, the other half are Caucasians including immigrants (and their descendants) from all over the Muslim World. The same variety of ethnic and cultural types can be witnessed in any convention of the Muslim Students' Association of the United States and Canada, the dominant and guiding Muslim organization in the North American continent.

WHAT IS A MUSLIM?

Every law court of Islam is bound to recognize as a Muslim in good standing, and hence entitled to all privileges and rights of a Muslim and bound by all the duties and obligations of Islamic law, every adult male and female who consciously and solemnly witnesses that "there is no God but God and Muhammad is the Prophet of God." Fulfillment of this simple definition of "Islamicity" is all that Islamic law requires for membership in the Muslim community. Once a person is put to the test and witnesses responsibly to the twin declarations of God being the only God and Muhammad being His Prophet, no more can be legally required as proof of faith and, consequently, that person enjoys all the rights and is obligated by all the duties under Islamic law.

The reason why "Islamicity" is so simple to define, so simple to attain, and so simple to establish, is that Islam is neither an ethnocentric nor a sacramental religion. One does not have to be born a Muslim; nor does one have to have any Muslim parent, guardian, family, or people. Every person in the world may become a Muslim if he or she so chooses, by a personal decision alone. Initiation into Islam needs no sacramental ceremony, no participation by any clergy, and no confirmation by any organized body. Therefore, all people are absolutely equal in that the house of Islam may be entered by everyone after satisfying the simplest of requirements. In the matter of people being Muslims or non-Muslims, there is no middle ground, no ambiguity, no complication.

Great as it may be in the eyes of Islam for any person to make the decision to enter the faith, the entry constitutes no guarantee of personal justification in the eyes of God. Since Islam has no sacraments, there is nothing the new initiate can do which would assure him or her of salvation.

In Islam, it is believed that God judges people by their deeds or works, not by rites or ceremonies such as baptism. Islam further denies that a human can attain religious felicity on the basis of faith alone. Faith, it says, is something one must have to enter into the community of Islam. One must declare this faith. But this faith may be only a mark of social self-identification. It may or may not produce the works of virtue, the deeds of righteousness. And only the works and deeds constitute justification in God's eyes.

On the scale of virtue and righteousness, people occupy varying positions. The scale itself is infinite; and there is no point at which Muslims may carry their titles to Paradise, as it were, in their pockets. Everyone strives and some strive more than others. God's judgment of a person's fate is not preempted by anything that an individual can do, whether for or against salvation. For God may reject the greatest deeds because of lack of faith and seriousness on the part of their doer, and He may forgive the greatest sinner. The Muslim, therefore, is a person who, having joined the ranks of Islam by solemn declaration, is engaged in the pursuit of righteousness for the rest of his or her life. Thus the simple test of "Islamicity" provided by Islamic law is balanced by a requisite for salvation which is by nature infinite and hence never fully satisfied. Religious justification is thus the Muslims' eternal hope, never their complacent certainty, not for even a fleeting moment.

Muslims, therefore, are people who, as they have solemnly declared, believe that only God is God and Muhammad is His Prophet. Believing that only God is God makes Muslims the humblest and at the same time the proudest creatures. They are humble and rub their foreheads against the ground before God. God is to them the One Creator,

Provider, Ruler, Forgiver, Judge, the First Cause and the Final End of everything, the Ultimate Reality. He is the object of adoration and praise, of thanks and worship, the One Master to Whom all one's life is devoted in dedication and service. The Muslim is the proudest of people precisely because of this loyalty to God. Besides God, no thing and no human is worthy of one's loyalty, of one's service and work. The Muslim may not submit to any ruler, and much less to any tyrant, because submission is due only to the One Master. Some Muslims indeed do submit to rulers and tyrants, but they do so at the cost of violating the very essence of their faith. But in submission to God, Muslims place themselves on a par with the rest of humankind which they believe is equally obliged to recognize God as Creator of all.

Muslims have a feeling of strong brotherhood to all who submit themselves to the Divine Sovereign; for in relation to the Creator, there is no perspective or bond mightier and more proper than that of being human creatures. Here all humans stand absolutely identical in their *creatureliness*. On account of their acknowledgment of God alone as Master, Muslims are revolutionaries who champion the cause of human freedom against *human* masters everywhere. Nothing is more hateful to them than associating other beings with God. When people set up money, sex, power, or pleasure as their God beside God, it is deplorable. But when a tyrant sets himself up and demands absolute loyalty from the citizens—loyalty belonging exclusively to God—then rebellion against that ruler and his ultimate overthrow become, for the Muslims, a prime religious objective.

The Muslim believes that God has created humankind and the world not in sport, and certainly not in vain, but for a purpose. This purpose is that humans may fulfill their ethical vocation—that they may do good deeds. The scripture of Islam pictures the life of humans as a free competition among them for doing the better, the nobler, the greater deeds. On this account, it called the individual a *khalifah,* or vicegerent (deputy) of God, that is, one who acts on behalf of God. The world God created is one which fits this moral vocation of humans. It is one in which they are effective, where the realization of goodness, truth, and beauty is actually possible.

Having just returned from their pilgrimage to Makkah (Mecca), these Nigerian Muslims line up in rows to pray.

This purpose is what gives meaning to the Muslim's life. And there can be no greater meaning than to fulfill and make real God's will on earth. It is the source of Muslim dignity and self-esteem. In fact, it assigns to the Muslim a cosmic status to see his or her person, on a par with all other people, as the bridge through which the moral good must pass to be actualized on earth. Realization of the moral good requires that it be achieved in freedom, that is, under the conditions where it is equally possible to realize as well as to violate the moral imperative. Of all creatures on earth, only humankind is so equipped.

To be a *khalīfah,* or vicegerent of God on earth, is no little burden. First, the task is worldwide. Everything in creation is an object for improvement. This means that the task involves the turning of every corner of the earth into all that it ought to be, namely, into a paradise. Equally, it means that upon the Muslim falls the task of educating and transforming humanity—not only oneself, one's children, next of kin, or compatriots—and of helping each of them to fulfill his or her personal potential. All the problems of humankind are hence the Muslim's problems. To accept them, to seek morally worthy solutions to them, and to work out these solutions—these tasks are the Muslim's obligation and destiny, as well as the Muslim's pride. Islam wants people to confront these problems head-on. It assures them that God will grant merit, and hence reward and happiness, in direct proportion to their commitment to the task, to their engagement in the job, to their success in achieving the divine purpose of creation—namely, the universal and highest good of all peoples and of all things. All of the Muslim's life is to be lived in service to God—that is, in educating and disciplining oneself, in discovering the laws of nature so as to make one's enjoyment of it possible and easy, and, finally, in living and enabling every person and thing to live the divine pattern which is God's will. Thus the Muslim is one who interferes with every natural process so as to make it serve human needs and fulfill human joys, who interferes with the life of everyone on earth so as to enable people to fulfill their potential and to realize their noble destiny as God's vicegerents. Obviously, to live the life of Islam is to live dangerously. But Muslims believe it is also to live with the highest expectation, the greatest promise, the deepest joy of which humans are capable.

WHY IS THE MUSLIM A MUSLIM?

That God is sole Creator and Master of the world, that He is the First Cause and Final End, that humans are His servants, that human service consists of kneading and molding the world and people into what it and they ought to be, and that not only is such service possible but the well-being and happiness of humanity depends on it—all this is Islam's view of reality. This view is not without grounds and justification, nor is it devoid of problems.

The first striking characteristic of Islam is that its view is wholly positive. It seems to prescribe the doing of good, and trusts that the moral imperatives can and will be obeyed. But are not humans by nature inclined to do the opposite, to do evil? Is it not human nature to sin, defy God, and disobey the moral commandments? Are not humans "fallen" creatures in need of ransom and salvation before they can be expected to do good?

That people are by nature inclined to sin and to defy and disobey God is certainly true, answers Islam. But, Islam claims, it is equally true that people's nature is also inclined to obey God, to do good and act ethically. The two are possible for them, and they incline to the one as much as they do to the other. The fact that one can do evil but instead does good, and can do good but rather does evil, adds a new dimension to the person's worth or worthlessness when one does either. If one were compelled—that is, without freedom—to follow a single course, the action would be neither moral nor immoral, though it might realize a material value or disvalue. Individuals are not hopelessly bound to one or the other course of action. If they were, they would not be considered morally responsible.

Therefore, in the Islamic view, human beings are no more "fallen" than they are "saved." Because they are not "fallen," they have no need of a savior. But because they are not "saved" either, they need to do good works—and do them ethically—which alone will earn them the desired "salvation." Indeed, *salvation* is an improper term, since, to need "salvation," one must be in a predicament beyond the hope of ever escaping from it. But men and women are not in that predicament. Humans are not ethically powerless. They are not helpless puppets capable of neither good nor evil. They are capable of *both*. To "save" themselves by deeds and works is their pride and glory. To miss the chance and pass all the opportunities by is pitiable neglect; to miss the calling deliberately and to do evil is to earn punishment, to deserve damnation.

Islam teaches that people are born innocent and remain so until each makes him or herself guilty by a guilty deed. Islam does not believe in "original sin"; and its scripture interprets Adam's disobedience as his own personal misdeed—a misdeed for which he repented and which God forgave.

Rather than demoralize people by declaring them all born with necessary, inescapable sin, Islam reassures them. It declares that God,

Who does not work in vain, has created people who are all fitted for the job as His vicegerents on earth. He has given them eyes and ears, the senses of touch, taste, and smell. He has given them a discerning mind and heart, imagination and memory, all to the end of discovering and understanding the divine pattern in creation. He built human beings as He did—with grasping fingers, hurrying feet, springing muscles, and supporting bones—to the end that they may manufacture, grasp, or produce what they need. He placed them on an earth that is receptive to their efficacy, where they can get things done. Finally, He gave them mastery over the whole of creation, for He made everything subservient to human beings. Even the sun, the moon, and the millions of stars were created expressly for the benefit of humankind. Instead of being damned before they walk on earth, Islam teaches that people are blessed with all these "perfections," with life and mastery over all things, and hence are all the more expected to fulfill the divine will in their lives.

Islam denies, therefore, that God had to ransom humanity by means of oblation and sacrifice. Such a view, it holds, does violence to both God and humanity, compromising the transcendence of the former and the moral status of the latter. Islam does regard Jesus as God's prophet, sent to teach identically the same message as all other prophets and to reform the Jews who had gone astray from the same teaching delivered to them by earlier prophets. It holds the Christians, not Jesus, accountable for what is being taught in his name. But it reassures them that they are essentially in the right, especially when they call people to worship God and to serve Him by doing good works. Moreover, Islam explains the Christians' "mistake" as due to the loss of the authentic texts of revelation. Profiting from their experience, Islam feels it has preserved the absolute integrity and authenticity of its own revealed text, explaining that God Himself has sent it down and that He alone is its guardian and keeper.

If all prophets have conveyed one and the same message, whence come all the religions of history? Assuming that they are genuine, Islam answers that there can be no difference in the messages of the prophets since their source is one, namely, God. Revelation through the prophets constitutes a fund of truth for every people, because God made His will known to every people in their own language. But Islam asserts that variations of space and time, acculturation by alien influences, and human whims and passions caused people to slip from the truth. The result was that the religions of history all erred more or less from the truth because none has preserved the original text of its revelation. In their pristine purity, the revelations were one and the same and contained the same principles of religion and ethics. If they differed at all, they did so only in the method they prescribed for achieving those essential principles. They were one in their "what," but many in their "how." The former is their core and essence and is universal and eternal; the latter is accidental and depends on the circumstances of history, on the peculiarities of the specific people to whom it was sent.

Paralleling the eternal "what," Islam claims, is a built-in capacity in all human beings to recognize God and to grasp His will as their moral duty. This is not merely human endowment with the senses and reason mentioned earlier. Besides all these, Muslims believe there is a sixth sense which all people share in common and which enables them to perceive God. There is no person without religion, and no religion without the holy. If people see the holy in different forms, that is due to their upbringing, their legacies of culture and religion. In its pure form, the sense of the supernatural in every person makes him or her aware of God, the Holy One, and of His will as the moral imperative. It is hence for more than one reason that God holds all humans equally responsible before Him.

Conversely, individuals ought to regard and treat all other people as equals. In acting morally, that is, in fulfilling the divine will, men and women should aim at the whole of humankind. Certainly considerations of nearness and strategy impose upon one to start good works at home, beginning with oneself. But granted these necessities, one cannot discriminate between the human creatures of God. Whether as subjects of moral action, or as objects of moral action by others, all humans are equal because they are all equally human creatures. And because they are creatures of God, they are obliged to serve Him. Universalism is God given as well as God commanded.

Within the Semitic family of nations in which Islam was born, the Jews have admirably preserved the revealed teaching that God is transcendent and One. However, Islam charged them with misunderstanding divine transcendence on two counts: first, when their scripture spoke of God in the plural form—*Elohim*—and reported "them" as marrying "the daughters of men";[6] second, when they thought of God as related to themselves in a way other than He is related to all other creatures, namely, as their father. Their teaching of a doctrine of divine election or "chosen people," which put them ahead of all people in receiving God's favors, Islam found objectionable. Jews held themselves to be God's children and elect, regardless of their deeds. In so doing they were subject to Islam's castigation and chastisement. Islam

---

[6] Genesis 6:2, 4.

regarded itself as the religion of Abraham, Jacob, Moses, and David as each of them conveyed the revealed message in its pure and unadulterated form. In consequence, Muslims identified themselves with the Jews as worshippers and servants of one and the same transcendent God and regarded their own religious doctrine as Judaism purged of all ethnocentrism and, especially, of the doctrine of "chosen people." As far as Jewish law and ethics are concerned, Islam confirmed the revelation of Jesus insofar as it removed the yoke of literalism and legalism which the Jewish tradition had spun around the Law of Moses, and revoked the laws which the rabbis had added to it.

Religious authority, Islam held, belongs only to God. As tyrants are condemned and people are commanded to shake off their tyranny, the road to God should be an open and free highway, admission to which has only one requisite—being a human creature. Islam declared that the priesthood and all its orders should be abolished. The tasks of teaching the truth, guiding the young, and counseling the erring will last as long as humankind. But, Islam held, these universal duties apply equally to all people. Prestige in the discharge of these tasks belongs to whoever has acquired the most and highest learning which is itself open to all. The ages-long occupation of priests as intermediaries between God and humankind is unnecessary in Islam.

Islam holds that human worship reaches to God without need for intermediaries. No aspect of God's power or divinity is channeled anywhere without threat to divine transcendence. God's power and sanctity are solely God's. They are not dispensed to any creature because Creator and creature are two absolutely different kinds of being which never fuse into each other. God is the Forgiver, Punisher, Judge, and Master, not the priest. He does not delegate these functions to any creature because that would violate His transcendence and role as sole Governor and Judge of humanity. He is fully responsive to every person's prayer. His mercy and care for humankind, along with His omnipotence, demand that all people address themselves directly to Him. God needs no bureaucracy. He is in direct control of human affairs; and worshippers, thanksgivers, confessors, and supplicators can all address themselves directly to the divine Presence.

It is God Who indeed is the Master, the sole Master. He alone is the Judge, and He knows all since nothing escapes His mastery. It is not in any human's power to dispense His power. Judgment of an individual's whole life, or of any of its deeds, is God's prerogative, not that of humans. And it is the consummating conclusion of human life when, on the Day of Judgment, every person is meted out the exact reward or punishment he or she has earned in life. In the view of Islam, the "other world" or the "other kingdom" or "heaven" has no other meaning than this consummation. It is not another world, another space-time designed to supplant this world; nor is it a replica of this world with all its deficiencies and shortcomings changed into perfections and fulfillments. Reasserting the essential innocence and goodness of both people and the world, Islam teaches not only that the realization of the good is possible in this world but that to bring it about here and now is precisely the duty of every man and woman. It warns humankind that there is no world other than this, that there is no space-time other than this, that all human duties and hopes are to be fulfilled in this world—if they are to be fulfilled at all. Since this world is itself God's creation and work, the Muslim believes that it is the realm in which perfection, the Divine will, utopia, or the absolute good may be realized. Islam believes that God created humans that they may achieve the good. Hence, it reasons, the good must be possible to actualize—indeed obligatory. Accordingly, Islam does not need another world for the good to be realized therein. Its "other world" is only a reward or punishment incurred by humans in accordance with their deeds.

Only such a view, Islam holds, is consistent with loyalty to this world. Without it, this world would become merely a bridge or passage on which people are transients, advised neither to tarry nor to build but quickly to get to the other shore. Such a view is a denial of this world. Islam, on the other hand, is world affirming, stressing this as the only world. People either succeed or fail in it, doing the right or the wrong. Because people are free and responsible, everything they do in this world counts for or against them. On the Day of Judgment, which will also be the termination of this world, they will be given what they have deserved—blessedness or damnation. Piety and morality, that is, obedience to God, bring happiness and acknowledge utopia in this world; at the same time they promise blessedness on the Day of Judgment. That is why Islam, Muslims hold, achieves for humanity two happinesses: happiness here and happiness in the Hereafter.

SINCE WHEN IS ANYONE A MUSLIM?

Islam began as a world religious movement in the first decade of the seventh century C.E. in the city of Makkah (Mecca) in Arabia. It was taught by Muhammad, son of 'Abdullah, of the tribe of Quaraysh and the clan of Hashim. When Muhammad was forty years old, he began to have visions in which God sent down a series of revelations through the Angel Gabriel. The revelations, recited in Arabic form, were a disclosure not of God, but of His will or commandments.

The revelations came piecemeal, sometimes asserting God's existence, His unity and providence, His judgment on the Last Day, sometimes describing what should be done in a situation which called for a solution, dispensation, or guidance. Sometimes the revelations applied to a situation with a wider religious context such as relations with unbelievers, or with Christians and Jews, of whom there were many in Arabia and the adjoining countries. At first Muhammad himself did not believe. He thought he was having illusions or was being tempted or possessed by the devil. But the visions persisted and the revelations continued, and he finally became convinced that God was truly calling him to rise and teach the new faith.

The first convert was Muhammad's wife, Khadijah. She became convinced, even before Muhammad, that he was indeed a prophet. Other relatives and friends began to believe in him also, and a nucleus community was formed. The Arabs, whose traditional faith was pagan, denied the unity and transcendence of God as well as the Day of Judgment. At first they reacted to the new teaching with scorn. But Muhammad and his companions stood firm. Then the unbelievers countered with public abuse, slander, and persecution.

The fledgling community bore its travail with patience and determination and continued to grow. Soon the Arab hierarchy in Makkah decided that there was no escape from total war against the new Muslims if the position of Makkah and its rulers in the religious, social, political, and economic spheres was to be saved. They offered Muhammad wealth and the kingship of Makkah, and promised to cure his "madness" by the greatest physicians of the world. But he refused. Then they sought to break up the tribal solidarity of Muhammad's clan of Hashim on which the Muslims depended for intertribal security. They appealed to the Prophet's uncle and personal protector—the non-Muslim Abu Talib, the clan's elder statesman—to renounce his tribal solidarity with Muhammad. The old uncle pleaded with his nephew to cease causing difficulties because the clan could no longer bear them. But the Prophet replied: "If the sun was put in my right

A street in modern Makkah, with the minarets of the Sacred Mosque in the background.

hand and the moon in the left in exchange for God's religion, I would never yield—not if I were to perish in preaching it!"

The Makkans finally decided Muhammad would have to be assassinated. But sensing danger, Muhammad had already arranged with Muslim converts in Madinah (Medina), a city some 250 miles to the north, to furnish him protection in case of need. When danger came close, he outwitted his enemies and slipped out of Makkah and escaped to Madinah. This move, called the Hijrah (emigration), marks the first year of the Muslim calendar, which corresponds to the year 622 of the Christian calendar.

Madinah was now reinforced with the Muslims of Makkah who had emigrated there, one after the other, on the advice of the Prophet. However, the danger there did not disappear, but took a more ominous turn. Now a real war broke out between Makkah and Madinah involving all the tribes of the countryside which the two powers could rally to their sides. Upon arrival in Madinah, Muhammad integrated the Muslims of all tribes into one solid body, and integrated this body with the Jews of Madinah to form an Islamic state. He gave it a constitution and assumed its leadership. The revelations continued to come, providing guidance in the social, political, economic, and judicial affairs with which Muhammad had to deal. The war with Makkah began with skirmishes followed by two great battles, one of which was gained by each party; but neither win was conclusive enough to enable the victor to put a final end to the hostility. A truce followed, before and during which Islam won the adherence of thousands. When allies of Makkah violated the truce, the Muslims mobilized and marched on Makkah, conquering it without a fight. In a noble gesture Muhammad forgave the Makkans, and they converted to Islam *en masse*. The Prophet entered the Ka'bah, the house which, according to tradition, Abraham and his son Ishmael built for worship of the One God and which had by then become filled with hundreds of idols. He destroyed the idols and cleansed and reconsecrated the house to God.

One campaign after another was launched to bring Islam to the remaining tribes of Arabia. Some tribes now felt free from the might of pagan Makkah and thus free to give conscientious consideration to the call of Islam. These joined the ranks of Islam voluntarily. Others felt strong enough to continue the fight without Makkah, and they had to be brought into line by force. Converts to Islam, however, did not come only from pagan Arabian religion. Arab Christians and Jews also converted. Those who rejected Islam and stood firm by their old faith, whether Judaism or Christianity, were not molested. On the contrary, under divine sanction revealed in the Qur'an, the Prophet had recognized Christianity, Judaism, and the religion of the Sabaeans[7] as revealed and valid. Muslims fraternized with followers of these religions and integrated them within the Islamic state, but allowed them to preserve their religion, their culture, their customs, and their non-Muslim identities. The Islamic state was their protector. They lived under its protection as religious, cultural, and legally autonomous units. They were complete communities with their own schools, temples, law courts, and leaders. Muhammad died in 632 of the Christian calendar—ten years after his Hijrah (emigration) to Madinah. But by then he left the whole of Arabia united and ready to carry the message of Islam to the world.

Muhammad had previously sent messengers to the leaders of the then-known world, inviting them to join Islam or, if they wished, to keep their religion but join the new world order of Islam which was being built on the principle of free movement of humans, ideas, and wealth. Few leaders accepted the invitation. Some answered with friendship and sympathy; others beheaded the messengers.

Then began one of the most spectacular conquests in human history. The Muslims burst out of Arabia and swept west across North Africa and east across Persia, reaching Spain and France in the west and India and China in the east. Within one hundred years the Islamic Empire stretched from the Atlantic Ocean to India, covering much of the Mediterranean world. Within a generation after Muhammad, millions of men and women had converted to Islam.

The great appeal of Islam consisted in the beautiful simplicity of its theological claim. The world was created by God, the one and only Transcendent Being who had created an orderly cosmos. He also created humankind as rational, free, and responsible individuals, able to improve the world by exercising human faculties.

To many, Islam seemed a happy religion. According to Muhammad, all people, regardless of race or degree of wealth, are brothers and sisters and are regarded as equals. God did not want people to mortify themselves or to lead lonely lives in monasteries. Rather He wanted them to live an abundant life, full of joy and happiness but always observing the moral laws of purity and faithfulness to God and showing fairness, love, and brotherhood.

But what really won millions of hearts to Islam was the fact that the Muslims really seemed to practice what they preached. There was little hypocrisy or racial prejudice. Muslims readily intermarried with the

---

[7]People living in the kingdom of Saba' in pre-Islamic southwest Arabia or those who are also called "Mandeans" living to this day in South Iraq.

citizens of other lands even before their conversion to Islam. But when a decision to join Islam was voiced by any non-Muslim of however lowly an origin or status, he or she was instantly raised to the highest level, declared a brother or sister to all believers, intermarried with them, and was welcomed into the Islamic community.

The Muslims took great pains to live by their faith. This instilled in the hearts of non-Muslims a deep sense of respect and admiration for Islam's followers. It also created a desire to emulate or join them.

Chapter 2

Moments of the Muslim's Religious Life

The five pillars of Islam—the five religious duties that constitute the fundamental obligations of Islam—are the subject of this chapter. They are (1) the confession of faith, (2) worship, (3) wealth sharing, (4) fasting, and (5) pilgrimage to the Ka'bah, the House of God, in Makkah.

THE SHAHADAH
(The Confession of Faith)

The Muslim confesses that there is no God but God and that Muhammad is the Prophet of God. This confession is the *shahadah,* or "witness." It is not only the Muslim's legal passport into the Muslim community but also the quintessence of the Muslim's faith and an expression of identity. This confession of faith is recited many times a day on many different occasions. The meanings implicit in its first half—"There is no God but God"—were elaborated in Chapter 1, in the section headed "What Is a Muslim?" Here, the contents of the second half—namely, "Muhammad is the Prophet of God"—are explored.

To assert the second half of the confession is to accept Muhammad's revelations as really coming from God. These revelations or sayings constitute the Holy Qur'an, the scripture of Islam, the commandments and directives God has given for the conduct of life on earth. Collected and set down in the Qur'an in the order in which the Prophet declared that they should be recited, these revelations constitute for the Muslim God's ever-present pronouncement.

To confess that Muhammad is the Prophet of God is tantamount to declaring that the Qur'an is indeed the holy word of God, complete, verbatim (word for word exactly), and in the order set forth by the Prophet. It also means the confessor believes that the Qur'an's commandments and directives are God's norms and standards of behavior to which Muslims must conform.

The authenticity and integrity of the text of the Qur'an, however, are beyond question. The Qur'anic revelations were both written down and memorized by millions. They are continuously recited in public throughout the Muslim World. Believing they are reciting the very words of God, Muslims have always given the recitation and copying of the Qur'anic text the most scrupulous care.

Normally the act of worship, the formal prayer, may not be interrupted for any reason—not even by a threat to the worshipper's safety—because in prayer the Muslim is supposed to stand in the presence of God. But worship *may* be interrupted by anyone listening, if the worshipper makes an error in the recitation of the Holy Qur'an.

Finally, at the very time that 'Uthman (the third caliph, or head of the Islamic community) was promulgating the present text of the Qur'an as a book, internal strife and contest for power split the community asunder. For centuries, the factions continued their bloody strife, each justifying its case with arguments and quotations from the Holy Book. Yet never has any one faction accused the other of tampering with the text. This was a final test of fire which the Qur'anic text has passed with flying colors. That is why the noted scholar Sir William Muir approvingly agreed with other scholars that "we are as certain that the Qur'an is the historical word of Muhammad as the Muslim is certain it is the word of God."[1]

The prophethood of Muhammad, restricting itself to the verbatim conveyance of the word of God, presents a capstone of the whole phenomenon of prophecy in Semitic culture. Certainly Moses represented another apex in that history, after which, Muslims believe, prophecy degenerated in Israel to the point of there being many false prophets loose in the marketplaces without any being able to prove his prophethood conclusively.

Islam reinstated prophecy to its place of high honor. The change in times, however, prescribed that prophets no longer justify themselves with miracles which boggle the mind. Hence, Muslims do not claim any miracles for Muhammad. In their view, what proves Muhammad's prophethood is the sublime beauty and greatness of the revelation itself, the Holy Qur'an, not any inexplicable breaches of natural law which confound human reason or pass the human powers of understanding. The Qur'anic revelation is a presentation to one's mind, to reason. It makes its claim critically, not authoritarianly. Instead of commanding blind belief, it invites people to consider the evidence, to

---

[1]Paraphrased from Sir William Muir, *The Life of Mohammad* (Edinburgh: John Grant, 1923), p. xxviii.

compare and contrast the claims and the data, and to judge only in certainty and conviction of the truth.

This is why Islam never had a religious synod or council or church empowered with the right to impose its own views about Islam on the rest of humankind. In Islam, religious truth is a matter of argument and conviction, a cause in which everybody is entitled to contend and everybody is entitled to convince and be convinced. To witness that Muhammad is the Prophet of God means in final analysis that one is convinced that religious truth is critical, arguable, and convincing of itself. This affects the first part of the *shahadah,* namely, "There is no God but God." It tells the Muslim that this is a rational claim, and one can be convinced of its truth without authority or coercion. One has to reason, to consider all the evidence, in seriousness and responsibility.

SALAT (Worship)

The word *salat* is better translated as "worship" than as "prayer." Prayer is not necessarily formal. It is not obligatory, has no prescribed style, and can be recited almost anywhere, anytime. Islam knows a form of communion with God which fits the appellation "prayer," and it is called *du'a',* literally "invocation" or "calling." Like "prayer," it varies according to the content, as in prayer of thanksgiving, of praise, of supplication, of forgiveness, and so on.

Unlike *du'a', salat* has a definite and precise form. It must be recited five times a day at given intervals. If the time assigned to it is missed, it can be made up, but with the understanding that one is only making up what has been missed. *Salat* is an absolute commandment of God imposed upon all adult Muslims. To deny it is to leave Islam. To neglect it is to commit a grave sin which must be repented and made up.

Salat is preceded by ablution—that is, the body, or parts of it, is washed. This ablution is both real and symbolic, and both levels of meaning are required in Islam. The Muslim may not approach the divine Presence, as one does in *salat,* with a dirty body or appearance. Just as the place where one prays must be clean (and hence the ubiquitous "prayer" rug throughout the world of Islam), so one's clothing and body must be equally clean. Soiled clothes have to be changed. Hands, mouth and teeth, nose, face, top of head, neck, ears, arms to the elbows, and feet to the ankle—all have to be washed in clean, preferably running, water. The whole operation must be preceded with a silent declaration of intention to oneself that one is entering into it for the sake of God.

As far as physical cleanliness is concerned, ablution is a welcome exercise. Its value can be appreciated when applied to people in the desert where dust abounds and to farmers in irrigated lands where mud is the order of the day, every day. But its blessings can also be appreciated in industrial cities where soot and other air-polluting agents threaten the citizens. Psychologists everywhere would probably applaud its refreshing and rejuvenating effect as it comes at dawn, noon, midafternoon, sunset, and night. As to its symbolic meaning, the ritual of ablution serves as self-preparation for communion with God.

Salat can be performed anywhere; for wherever the Muslim stands, there is God present. No ground is holy; the mosque is a place dedicated to worship, but not "consecrated." *Salat* can be performed by the worshipper alone, since there is no sacrament and no priesthood in Islam. Performing it together with one's fellow worshippers is desirable but not obligatory except for the congregational *salat* on Friday *(Jum'ah)* which must be performed with the other members of the congregation. The congregational *salat* is led by an *imam* (leader) whose function is to synchronize the movements of beginning and ending, of genuflection and prostration. Any Muslim may lead the *salat,* provided one's recitation of the Qur'an is correct. On Friday, the *imam* delivers a *khutbah,* or sermon, in addition to these duties. The subject of the sermon should be a living issue in Muslim life, and the *imam* should try to relate the relevant passages of the Qur'an and *hadith* (report of the example of the Prophet's behavior) to the problems or situation at hand.

For the congregational *salat,* the Qur'an advises that beautiful clothes be worn with decorum. Before starting, the *imam* makes sure that the lines of worshippers are full and solid and straight. All face in the direction of the Ka'bah in Makkah. The sight of Muslims in *salat,* whether standing in their straight rows or kneeling and prostrating themselves, is indeed a forcefully expressive and deeply moving sight. The straight line represents the equality of all; the rows represent the fullness and solidity of the community.

The night ends at dawn and the day begins. Islam prescribes that each day begin with *salat.* Between dawn and the noon *salat,* there is usually a period of seven to eight hours which can and should be used to do the day's work. Where the work is of a heavy nature, this period is adequate to satisfy the needs of a progressive, well-organized economy.

Muslims performing ablution in the courtyard
of the Umawi Mosque in Damascus, Syria.

Where the work is light, it can be resumed after the noon *salat,* which can also constitute a refreshing break. No one need work beyond the midafternoon *salat,* unless it is for an emergency situation or for one's own pleasure and desire. The sunset *salat* terminates the day, and the night *salat* marks the Muslim's retirement.

Salat is a discipline. Its ablution, its form, its movement, the timing and number of genuflections and prostrations—all these constitute exercises in self-attunement to the call of God. The Qur'an says that *salat* is futile unless it leads to moral action and self-exertion in the greater cause, the cause of God. It is supposed to be more than just a reminder of God. For its duration, five times a day, it is to bring people for a time face to face, as it were, with their Lord, Master, and Creator.

ZAKAT (Wealth Sharing)

Zakat, which literally means "sweetening," justifies or renders legitimate, innocent, and good that which it is supposed to affect. The term can be used with a human being as object, in which case it means recommendation or acclamation. When used with wealth as its object—and that is the greater usage—it means making that wealth "sweet" (just, legitimate, innocent, good, and worthy). Obviously, the worth *zakat* adds to wealth is not utilitarian, but moral.

Islam regards all wealth as belonging to God. One may appropriate as much of it as one pleases, by all the means which economic life makes possible, as long as such means do not violate the moral law. Wealth gathering is legitimate activity as long as it implies no theft, cheating, or coercion. Indeed, the pursuit of wealth is one of the primal concerns of humankind, demanded by survival (where it consists of the search for food, shelter, and clothing) as well as by a person's *khilafah,* or vicegerency (where its object is the planned satisfaction of one's own material needs and those of humanity). Engagement in such a pursuit fills the greatest portion of life and exhausts the greatest energies of all humans, everywhere and at all times. Wealth gathering is the very stuff of which living consists, but it must be subject to the moral law. Without this law, human life sinks to the level of the animals of the forest.

But even if the moral law has been strictly observed in every step of the process of acquiring wealth, that wealth still needs justification on another level. This is what the institution of wealth sharing, or *zakat,* seems to require. If one violates no moral law in acquiring wealth, why does Islam hold such wealth nonetheless illegitimate until one has justified it by means of *zakat?*

The answer is that while the moral law governs the acquisition of wealth, its consumption and/or continued possession must also be governed by moral considerations. Were there no purpose to life but existence, and no meaning to that existence except pleasure, comfort, and satisfaction, no demand could be made of the owner of wealth. But there is more to life than this.

Islam's tenet is that wealth, once acquired, ought to be shared with others in some proportion. This is equally the requirement of charity, and charity is as old as humanity. Charity has always been regarded as high moral value. Its proportion—nay, its very observance—has been left to the personal discretion of the giver. True, morality has always taught that the greater the portion one shares, the greater the merit. Jesus moved charity to higher moral grounds when he taught that the purer the motivation with which the giver gives his wealth, the greater the *moral* worth of the deed. With all this Islam fully agrees, recognizing this teaching of Jesus as genuine revelation from God. It called the institution of almsgiving *sadaqah,* a derivative from the act of faith itself by which people acknowledge God to be God.

No religion or morality before Islam has made charity itself obligatory in the sense of institutionalizing it and empowering somebody to levy, collect, and distribute it. It is nice to have charity as a moral ideal. But what would be its worth if it remained an unobserved ideal? An ideal satisfiable by the millionaire who gives a few pennies to the poor on the sidewalk? An ideal whose observance is subject only to one's conscience, or to God in the Hereafter, but to no regulation by one's peers in this world?

This is the need to which Islam addressed itself by the institution of *zakat:* "You may give your wealth to your fellow humans as much as you please, when you please, in the manner you please. That is your *sadaqah,* of which your conscience and God are the only judges. But you may not escape the requirement of giving every year two and one-half percent of your total wealth to a corporate institution, the Islamic state, for distribution to the less fortunate, to those in need." Thus, Islam sought to preserve the moral value of charity, and to add to it the equally moral value of wealth sharing, or *zakat.* Its purpose was dual: to convince the wealthy that the title to their wealth is mitigated by the title of their fellow humans to life and subsistence, and to assure the needy that their fellows will not passively see them suffer misfortune. A bond of humanity binds both the wealthy and the poor together. The Prophet said: "Men are like the organs of a body. When an organ suffers, the whole body responds to repel the cause of suffering." The Qur'an went so far as to equate the consciousness of the need for

altruistic self-exertion with religion itself: "Who is the denier of religion itself? It is he who repulses the orphan, who does not enjoin the feeding of the poor. Woe to those who observe the rituals of religion but are insensitive to the moral side of those rituals, and hence to the need of the most miserable for assistance" (Qur'an 107:1–7).

Being a tax on wealth, *zakat* is incumbent on all liquid, visible, movable and immovable properties belonging to Muslims. It does not matter whether the owner is minor or adult, male or female—indeed, alive or dead. The estate of a deceased person is taxable in the same way, before any creditors' claims against it are satisfied. Being a right of God, *zakat* is prior to any other right. Three principles govern the levying of *zakat*. First, no *zakat* is due on property intended for consumption, such as houses, gardens, clothing, or furniture. Jewelry of gold, silver, and precious gems is excepted because it may serve as a channel for hoarding wealth, which Islam condemns. Taxable property is that which is intended for production, whether industrial, agricultural, or commercial. Second, *zakat* is not an indiscriminate tax on all properties. Assessment of *zakat* must take into consideration the *net* income produced by the property in question. In a year of a losing operation, no *zakat* is levied on the property concerned. Third, a reasonable amount necessary for the owner and his dependents' subsistence must be deducted from the assessment.

SIYAM (Fasting)

Fasting is an old religious custom. It was practiced by lay persons and clergy in ancient religions, as well as by Jews and Christians. Though its purposes differed from religion to religion, there was general agreement that fasting was a self-preparation for communion with divinity.

Islam prescribes a rigorous fast (called *siyam* in Arabic) for all healthy adult Muslims. This fast requires total abstention from food, drink, and sex from dawn to sunset during every day of the month of Ramadan, the ninth month in the Islamic calendar, which is based on the lunar year. The body may not partake of anything in any way or contact another of the opposite sex without breaking the fast. Exempted from this duty are children and persons suffering from

A produce market in Tangiers, Morocco. Commercial crops are among the kinds of property on which zakat *is imposed.*

sickness or undergoing the tremendously heavy burden of desert travel. In such cases, the exempted person is not to forego the fast but to postpone it to another, healthier or more restful time before recurrence of the following Ramadan.

Long before Islam, the month of Ramadan was regarded by the Arabs as a holy month. Its occasion imposed upon them the prohibition of war and hunting, and brought about an uninterrupted peace during which travel and movement of goods across the desert were safe from attack. The Arabs reckoned Ramadan as the month of spiritual stocktaking. Throughout its duration, they were especially keen to please, to settle old debts and disputes, to do good to their neighbors. The more morally sensitive among them underwent a retreat to a temple, or into their homes, to avoid disturbing their concentration and meditation. Before his commission as Prophet, Muhammad was in the habit of retreating during Ramadan to Hira', a cave outside Makkah, where he would spend several days in meditation. His wife used to send him daily provisions with a servant, knowing that her husband was devoting himself exclusively to worship.

Islam continued the tradition of dedicating the month of Ramadan to religious pursuits. Besides the fast, the Islamic tradition regarded moral and religious action during Ramadan as especially meritorious, and urged Muslims to increase their service to God during the month. It was during Ramadan that Muhammad received his first revelation.

Islam assigned two purposes to fasting: self-discipline and commiseration with the hungry of the earth. We have seen that Islam repudiates self-mortification and asceticism. Islam does not believe that righteousness requires humankind to deny itself. God wishes people to be free, healthy, fulfilled, and happy. As philosophers might put it, going to the dentist is certainly a painful experience. One does not undergo pain for its own sake unless one assumes that suffering is the end of human life. One endures pain willingly, however, if one believes it will lead to health and well-being which are the opposite of suffering. Accordingly, there is no denying that fasting is a hardship, so to what purpose did Islam impose it? To understand the purpose is to understand Ramadan.

Self-discipline through fasting is a novel religious idea. Hunger and sexual desire are pivotal instincts of life. Their satisfaction is a capital requirement of any social order. But they are precisely two of the most sensitive areas of human life. Prohibition of food and sex constitutes a threat to life, the former to individual life and the latter to group life. Deliberate abstinence from food and sex stirs up the consciousness of imminent death to both the individual and the group, and provides ample opportunity to mobilize consciousness and launch it into combat, in defense of life.

Islam has prescribed total abstinence from food and sex from dawn to sunset precisely for that reason. The threat to individual and group life must be resisted, and the Muslim must be taught and trained in the art of resistance. Patience, forbearance, perseverence, steadfastness in suffering and privation—these are the qualities Islam seeks to cultivate through fasting. Conversely, the areas of food and sex are regarded as two of humanity's weakest spots in regard to morality and righteousness. The Muslim sees them as avenues for vice and immorality to find their way into the world. To learn how to block those avenues of immoral use, fortify the individual against temptation, and make one's moral house impregnable is the purpose of Islamic fasting.

Hence, Islam looks upon fasting as the best exercise in the art of self-mastery. To make the exercise more effective, Islam prescribes that the fast be broken promptly at sunset, even before the performance of the sunset *salat.* Thus Islam regards every day in Ramadan as a fresh exercise or trial which, if carried successfully to sunset, may be ended with celebration, food, and joy, so that the abstinence—and hence the exercise—may be started all over again at dawn the next day. A little indulgence at night, the Legislator seems to have thought, might even make the daytime abstinence a better exercise in self-mastery than continuous denial which can quickly become habitual and hence of diluted effect. The alternation of abstinence and indulgence each day and night is thought to be more forceful and effective.

Throughout the Muslim World, the month of Ramadan is received with joy. People uphold the fast and literally change their countenances. No time is better for expressing the social bond uniting Muslim to Muslim. At night, Muslim towns and villages are alive with togetherness and merrymaking. Lest the latter get out of hand and cloud the moral lesson, Islam prescribes a special *salat* for the nights of Ramadan, namely, *tarawih.* Ideally this *salat,* which is at least as long as all the others of the day combined, involves the recitation of the whole Qur'an in successive parts during the twenty-nine or thirty days of the month.

The end of Ramadan is marked by a feast called *'Id al Fitr* (feast of the breaking of the fast) which Muslims celebrate with a congregational *salat* the first morning after Ramadan, and with gifts, visits with relatives and friends, food, and joyful events. New clothing for young and old is imperative for *salat* of the *'Id al Fitr,* which is held in as few places as possible so as to bring together the greatest possible number of Muslims in each place. The joy of the feast is a culmination of moral success at the daily fast of the previous month. If the trial of the month of Ramadan has been a success in its totality, the feast is well deserved. The Muslim would have emerged "proven" in his or her ability to bend pivotal forces of nature, the instincts for food and sex, to the demands of morality and religion. After a successful Ramadan, the Muslim must feel more capable and more ready to undertake any duty, any task. Like a bow, one has become tauter for the arrow.

The second purpose of fasting is commiseration with the hungry and deprived of the earth. Privation is without doubt humanity's constant and greatest affliction. There is no teacher more eloquent or effective than experience. For one to undertake the fast of Ramadan is to be reminded of and to sympathize with the deprived everywhere. To sharpen the lesson, Islam recommends to those who can afford it the voluntary act of feeding a neighbor, especially a poor one, every day of Ramadan, in further emphasis that Ramadan is *the* month of charity, of altruism, of neighborly love and kindness. It also prescribes, as personal atonement, the feeding of sixty persons for every day of Ramadan on which the fast is broken deliberately in defiance of God, and the feeding of two people (in addition to making up the fast on other days) if the fast is broken for legitimate reasons. Finally, it prescribes that no Muslim may attend the '*Id al Fitr salat* unless he or she has extended charity to the poor the previous night. This is *zakat al Fitr* (charity of fast ending). Its amount is prescribed to be the equivalent of two meals on behalf of each member of the household. This measure is designed to bring the joys of the feast to the poor and hungry as well.

This philosophy of fasting illustrates Islam's humanism and affirmation of this world. Fasting, the art of world-denial *par excellence,* practiced by the ascetics of all religions, is here transformed into an instrument of world affirmation. Rather than being a tool of self-denial for ascetics, fasting in Islam has become a tool of self-mastery for the better conduct of human life. The pursuit of this life and of this world is thereby ennobled and brought closer to righteousness through charity and obedience to God.

Pilgrim tents on the plain of Arafat during hajj. *The Mount of Mercy, marked by a white pillar denoting the spot where Muhammad stood to give his last sermon, is seen in the background.*

HAJJ (Pilgrimage)

Pilgrimage is the last of the five pillars of Islam, the religious duties which constitute the fundamental obligations of Islam. The pilgrimage to Makkah is incumbent only upon the adult Muslims who have earned the wealth needed for the trip, have paid the *zakat* ("sweetening") due on it, have fulfilled all their debts, and have provided adequately for all their dependents during their projected absence.

Once the decision to undertake it is reached, the pilgrimage begins with many celebrations and preparations at home. When the time comes for travel, the whole community goes out to bid the pilgrims farewell and wish them a pilgrimage acceptable to God. Upon arriving near Makkah al Mukarramah (Mecca the blessed), but before actually entering it, the pilgrims shed their clothes and ornaments, take a purifying ablution, and declare to God their *niyyah,* or intention, to perform the pilgrimage. Each pilgrim then puts on two pieces of unsewn white linen or cotton. One piece covers the body from the waist down, the other from the waist up, leaving the head bare. Henceforth pilgrims may not shave, cut their hair, clip their fingernails, or wear anything which might distinguish them from the other pilgrims. They can, of course, change their wraps, called *ihram,* for clean ones whenever they wish.

This clothing requirement is charged with religious meaning. The pilgrim, who comes to Makkah to meet the Creator, is a creature on a par with all other human creatures of God. Wealth, social class, political power, knowledge, wisdom, even previous piety—none of these is allowed to show itself. The distinctions of history are wiped out. All humans are creatures equal before God, and the wearing of *ihram* signifies this equality.

Pilgrims begin their ritual with a visit to the *haram,* an area about eighteen miles long and encompassing Makkah, the plain of Arafat, and other points sacred to Muslims. Immediately upon entering the sanctuary, the pilgrims proceed to the heart of Makkah where the Ka'bah stands. According to tradition, confirmed in the Qur'an, the Ka'bah was the first house of worship built for the worship of God. It was built by Abraham and his son Ishmael, whom the Arabs regard as their ancestors and Muslims regard as the first monotheists in the region. The pilgrims walk around the Ka'bah seven times while reciting a prayer affirming their submission to God's call.

The pilgrims then go on to Safa and Marwah, two little hills a bit less than a mile apart and also within the sanctuary. They cover the distance between the hills seven times at a trotting pace. This ritual, called *al sa'y* ("the striving"), is a symbolic reenactment of the experience of Hagar, Abraham's wife and the mother of Ishmael. At God's command, Abraham had left her in that locality with her newborn son. Anxious for the baby's safety and her own, she searched the area for water, running to and fro between the two hills. Hagar did eventually find water when, as tradition reveals, it sprang miraculously from under Ishmael's little feet. The fountain, called Zamzam, still gives its water to the pilgrims, many of whom take bottles of it to their relatives back home.

On the second day, the pilgrims begin their journey to Arafat, a plain a few miles northeast of Makkah where they camp. On the day of Arafat, the pilgrims stand together in prayer from the noon to the sunset *salat,* gathering around the very spot where Muhammad stood to deliver his farewell sermon on his last pilgrimage in the tenth year of the Muslim calendar (632 C.E.).

The pilgrims then proceed to Mina, an oasis eight miles away from Arafat, stopping to throw pebbles at one of three pillars that represents Satan. This is a condemnation of the devil and his ways and symbolically reaffirms the pilgrims' resolution to resist temptation.

At Mina the pilgrims buy a sheep or goat which they then sacrifice, giving the meat to the poor. This sacrifice, called the *'Id al Adha* (feast of sacrifice), is a high point of the pilgrimage, marking the pilgrims' willingness to sacrifice for God and to give thanks to Him, while also reminding the pilgrims that they should share with those who are less fortunate.

The most important parts of the pilgrimage are now complete, and at this point the pilgrims may take off the *ihram* and put on their usual clothes. They also clip their nails and hair as a sign of their partial return to everyday life.

But the pilgrimage is not yet ended. The pilgrims now return to Makkah, where they repeat *al sa'y* and once again walk seven times around the Ka'bah as they did at the beginning.

This concludes the pilgrimage itself, but most pilgrims also visit Madinah al Munawwarah (Medina the illuminated city of the Prophet) to pay their respects to the Prophet buried within its mosque. They then prepare to return home where relatives and communities will be waiting for them with a warm welcome and prayers that their pilgrimage has been accepted.

Failure to perform any of the rituals of pilgrimage because of sickness, accident, or death would not invalidate it; but failure to attend the standing at Arafat would, for that ritual is the core of the pilgrimage. Its simple meaning is evident in the invocation which the pilgrims recite then, as well as throughout the pilgrimage. Its refrain is *Labbayka Allahumma, Labbayka!* (At your call, O God, Here I come). God has called humanity to recognize Him as the One Creator and Lord, to obey His commandments, and to serve Him. The whole ritual is the pilgrims' affirmative response to that divine call.

Since the pilgrims affirm their recognition of God's creatorship, they also affirm all humankind's creatureliness and hence equality before God. The pilgrimage is therefore the greatest and most eloquent embodiment of Islam's egalitarianism and universalism. In 1977 C.E., over a million and a quarter Muslims performed the pilgrimage. Every year for the nearly fourteen hundred years since Muhammad's farewell pilgrimage, Muslims have gathered for the same ritual from the four corners of the earth. Here Muslims of all races, classes, cultures, and ways of life gather to reaffirm and renew their obedient and affirmative response to what they regard as God's call. *Hajj* is perhaps the most spectacular and moving religious event anywhere in the world. Certainly none has attracted so many people consistently and regularly over so many centuries.

CHAPTER 3

The Prophet Muhammad

The visit which pilgrims pay to Madinah and to the Prophet's grave is indicative of the honor and esteem in which the Prophet is held by all Muslims. The Muslim is always expected to invoke God's blessing on the Prophet whenever and wherever his name is mentioned. Such invocations are made a countless number of times a day, every day; and the *salat* includes it as part of the liturgy. This chapter deals with the impact of Muhammad's prophethood and with the celebrations commemorating special events in his life.

THE SPECIAL PLACE OF MUHAMMAD

There have been many prophets before Muhammad and many charismatic leaders who earned the love and admiration of their people; but none has commanded more love, honor, and respect from their followers than Muhammad. Some men commanded so much love and honor on the part of their adherents that the latter transformed them in their consciousness and declared them divine. The practice of deification was common in classical antiquity as well as in India, China, Japan, and Africa. One could even venture the suggestion that there is something in human nature that tends to associate with divinity anything that is perceived as sublime. Indeed, much as Islam condemned the practice, some of the Prophet's followers yielded to this temptation. As the Prophet lay on his deathbed, these clamored that he did not die but was lifted to heaven to join God's company. The denial of his mortality was the first step toward proclaiming him divine.

On hearing the news of the Prophet's death, Abu Bakr, his closest friend and constant companion, went into his room to see for himself what had happened. He then entered the mosque hall where the leader 'Umar was claiming that Muhammad had been lifted to heaven. After several polite but unsuccessful attempts to silence 'Umar, Abu Bakr stood up, shoved 'Umar aside, and said to the assembled Muslims: "If any of you has been worshipping Muhammad, let him know that Muhammad is dead. But if you have been worshipping God, then know that God is eternal and never dies." This was a terribly shocking reminder to the Muslims that only God is God, only He is immortal, and that Muhammad was human, all too human and mortal, like everyone else. It was the last time the Muslims entertained any idea of deifying the Prophet.

Muhammad's humanity is not a drawback, but an enhancement of his merit. His career would not be instructive had he been divine. People would then have to struggle with the translation of divine conduct into something humanly possible, capable of human actualization. But as a human, he received the revelation of God; and as a human, he conveyed it to humanity. As a human, he understood the revelation, interpreted and exemplified it in his life.

Islam holds that in His mercy, God sent a prophet to each and every people, and that all prophets have taught essentially the same lesson. If God cannot be subject to change, His will, the content of all revelations, must be the same. It is not fitting for an almighty and all-knowing God to change His will for humanity from place to place or age to age. Certainly the means of obedience by men and women may and did change, but not the religious or moral purpose of the divine commandment.

There is, however, a sense in which Muslims recognize that the divine commandment may change. That is when the commandment is not an imperative of goodness, justice, or charity but a prescription of how, in a concrete case, goodness, justice, or charity may be realized. Prescriptive religious laws do indeed change; for they are dependent upon the concrete situations in which they are to apply. But that is a change in the accidents of revelation, not in the substance. Islam recognizes that the requisites of history demand change but affect only the "how" of religion, never the "what." The succession of past prophets, Islam explains, was caused either by changing situations or by aberration and misunderstanding of the substance of revelation.

Muhammad, therefore, is not claimed by Muslims to have brought anything new to the revelations of past prophets. His revelation is a confirmation of all previous revelations. Moreover, the revelation to Muhammad—the Qur'an—is imperishable because God declared Himself its protector and guardian. Muslims have responded throughout the centuries by committing the Qur'an to memory so that it can never disappear from the earth. They have preserved the Arabic language, with all its grammar and syntax, so that an understanding of the language of revelation may forever be possible and easy.

Muslims hold the Qur'an to be essentially a statement of religious ends, of the "what" of divine will. They do not deny that the Qur'an does include some legislation, but they hold that element to be of lesser importance than the rest. Out of a total of 6,342 verses, hardly 500 are prescriptive, the rest being an exhortation to piety and virtue in general terms. They hold that God will not need to send another revelation, partly because He has placed in human hands an imperishable and definitive statement of His will, that is, the Qur'an, and partly because He wishes people themselves to discover and to elaborate the means by which the will of God is henceforth to be realized. It is not by accident therefore that the Qur'anic revelation is not prescriptive in the main; it is because the divine plan relegated lawmaking to humankind, as long as the principles and values that the prescriptive laws embody are those which God has revealed.

Muslims draw three important conclusions from this. First, there is no need for a prophet after Muhammad. That which might make another prophet necessary—namely, corruption or loss of revelation, or a change of situations requiring a corresponding change in prescriptions—cannot come to pass. The Qur'an is imperishable, and prescriptive legislation is the duty and prerogative of humankind. Second, Muhammad is the last of the prophets, sent not to a people, but to the whole of humanity. Third, as the model adherent of the religion he received from God, Muhammad is the exemplar of Islam; and his *sunnah,* or concrete example, sets the standard of behavior.

Muhammad was not therefore merely the messenger who conveyed the message of his Lord verbatim. He concretized, particularized, and specified the divine message. God had prepared him for the task, and his people never knew of a single flaw in his character. Hence it says in the Qur'an that Muhammad's conduct stands *par excellence* as the example for Muslim emulation. Muslims believe that two singular merits are therefore his by divine arrangement: verbatim delivery of the message and its concretization in life.

Both of these meanings are remembered, articulated anew, and celebrated on Muhammad's birthday, which falls on the twelfth day of the third lunar month of the Islamic calendar. On that day, Muslims celebrate the advent of Muhammad with a reading of his biography and with festivities for family and children. The *sunnah,* or example of Muhammad, is observed by Muslims in many events of every day. But on this day, Muslims are especially drawn to the realization of the need for this *sunnah* and of the tremendous effort that the Prophet's companions and their children, grandchildren, and great-grandchildren exerted in keeping it pure and unchanged. There was little trouble in preserving and conveying the text of the Qur'an, as we have already seen. Its language and style are so elegant and distinctive that not much training is needed to recognize it and separate it from other writings. But Muhammad's own language is like that of the rest of humanity.

Identifying authentic traditions of the Prophet was therefore a task demanding great care.

The *sunnah* has come down in reports, called *hadiths,* carried by the Prophet's companions and passed to the generations after them. Muslims are aware that the *sunnah* was tampered with as it was transmitted between the first four generations after Muhammad. Hence, Muslims are always careful to quality the *sunnah* with the word *al sahihah* ("veritable" or "verified"). To sift the veritable from the weak or spurious *hadiths,* Muslims developed the science of textual criticism and elaborated sophisticated disciplines to ascertain the historical reliability of each *hadith*—of the chain of narrators, of the form or language, of the editing of the text, of the coherence and rationality of the content of the text and its correspondence with the Holy Qur'an and with other historical reality and the accumulated wisdom of humankind. Using the disciplines of grammar, syntax, lexicography, etymology, philology, redaction, and literary aesthetics, the Muslims developed the tools of textual, form, topical, and historical criticism to examine the texts of the *hadiths.* They further developed other disciplines such as biography, historiography, and social analysis to investigate the truthfulness of the narrators of the *hadiths.* They established canons of both internal and external criticism for this task.

Their determination could not be absolutely definitive because of the nature of the case. Hence they did not throw away what they found falling short of absolute authenticity, but categorized it as such, reminding the reader that God knows better than they. Their researches did enable them to classify all the traditions of the Prophet's doing and saying according to their degree of authenticity in descending order. First are reports of an act of the Prophet which he taught Muslims to do and which they have performed repeatedly ever since. This is an "actional" *sunnah* and is hardly capable of error, considering its universal, repeated, and public nature. Second are those *hadiths* of juridical nature which had visible and public consequences in history and had thus been verified by the incontrovertible facts of that history. Third are those *hadiths* of a religious or moral nature which are obviously consistent with the Qur'an and were thus meant to

A decorated page from a fifteenth-century Qur'an.

illustrate or exemplify its ideas and injunctions. Last are those *hadiths* which carry some creative, innovative direction or tell something that is not reported by other known narratives or traditions.

Muslims look to the Prophet's *sunnah* under these categories. They are careful to call the Prophet's actions that are canonized by the Qur'an *al sunnah al sahihah* (the verified *sunnah*), thus keeping the door open for the possibility of human error. It is then imperative for human beings to remove error from the precincts of the divine will which, after all, really is religion.

THE PROPHET'S HIJRAH TO MADINAH

Important as the Prophet's birthday may be, it was not deemed by Muslims to be the proper beginning for the Islamic calendar. It must be kept in mind that Muhammad was not the first prophet, although Muslims regard him to be the last, in accordance with the divine description of him in the Qur'an as the "seal" or last of the prophets.

The coming of the Prophet indicates for Muslims a contact with divinity which brought humankind the knowledge of God's will. It also indicates preparation for the implementation of this will through the example of the Prophet. As such, the Prophet's coming signifies more for the divine timetable than for the human. It does not necessarily mark the commencement of the Islamic movement in history. The Islamic calendar had therefore to have another beginning.

It was 'Umar ibn al Khattab, the second caliph, who established the Islamic calendar as beginning on July 16, 622 C.E., the day of the Prophet's Hijrah, or emigration to Madinah. The reasoning is precise and clear. Islam is a divine dispensation meant to be an ideology for a comprehensive movement issuing from Makkah and enveloping the earth and humankind. When did it launch itself on this cosmic career? Not on Muhammad's birthday! Nor on the first day of revelation when the Prophet himself was not yet quite sure of what was happening. Nor on the emigration of some of the Prophet's companions to Ethiopia, for their flight was one of refugees. But on the emigration of the Prophet, or actually the day after, when he proclaimed the establishment of the Islamic state and launched Islam as a world movement and a cosmic mission.

Was such a launching necessary for the religion itself? Was it not an accident of history or a deliberate human pursuit and hence simply the result of something humans thought essential? No, answers the Muslim. God deemed it essential.

Involvement in history is essential to Islam and its ultimate end. For Islam is not a personalist, subjective religion, but rather one which urges humans to become involved in the process of history, to reorient its forces, humanity, and nature to remold the cosmos according to the pattern God has revealed. Muslims see their vocation precisely in this: to enter history and therein to reshape the world. Unlike those religions which define salvation essentially in terms of personal happiness or exaltation, Islam regards society—and hence its ordered form in the state—as absolutely necessary. In Islam, the community and all the institutions necessary for its health and discipline, its expansion and march, are vital for the transformation of humanity, nature, and the world.

All this is implicit in the Muslims' celebration of the Hijrah. It is a reminder of one year past and another to begin. It is a moment of stocktaking, not in the domain of personal life, but in that of public life where the subject is Islam as world movement, as world state. Every Muslim must ask: How close is the world movement the Prophet had launched in Madinah to realizing its God-given objective? How far is it from including and mobilizing humanity? From transforming that humanity into monuments of genius, heroism, and saintliness? From transforming nature into paradise?

THE PROPHET'S ISRA'-MI'RAJ

The Isra'-Mi'raj celebration commemorates Muhammad's night journey to Al Aqsa mosque in Jerusalem and his ascension from there to heaven (Qur'an 17:1). The occasion, which falls on the twenty-seventh day of the seventh lunar month, is celebrated by Muslims with prayers, sermons on the subject, and a vigil which ends with a banquet for the family and sweets for the children. The religious meaning of the celebration is, besides the institution of *salat,* Islam's recognition that Christianity, Judaism, and Islam are three religions of one family whose source is one and the same God.

As the youngest of world religions, and as one born in the cradle of both Judaism and Christianity, Islam could not help but relate itself to those two older religions. Its theory of prophecy bound Islam to recognize the prophethood of the Hebrew prophets as well as of Jesus, whose memories were very much alive in the Arabia of Muhammad's time. The Qur'an mentions many of them and pays particular attention to Abraham, Jacob, Midyan, Moses, David, Solomon, Jonah, and Jesus. It identifies them and their followers as *hanifs,* that is, Arabs who were neither Jewish nor Christian, nor adherents of the Makkan religion, and yet were held in utmost respect for their moral uprightness, religious vision, and spirituality. Islam had therefore to specify its relation to them.

The *hanifs* were regarded by Islam as the Arab carriers of the legacy of Semitic religious consciousness, from Sargon of Akkad to Abraham and Moses and finally to Jesus. Undoubtedly their ranks were swelled by those refugees who fled persecution in Palestine, Jordan, and Syria where the religious establishments often tried to enforce a particular version of orthodox Judaism or orthodox Christianity. In so doing, they produced recurrent waves of dissidents, some of whom found refuge among Arabs with similar views. In addition, there were Jewish refugees escaping the forced Hellenization of Alexander's heirs, and Christian refugees escaping Roman and Jewish persecution. This is borne out by the fact that *hanif* is the Arabic form of a Syriac word meaning "heretic," "rejected," or "separatist," exactly what such refugees would be from the establishment's point of view.

The *hanifs* regarded Abraham as their ancestor and asserted that he was the first *hanif*. The *hanifs* had no scripture, a fact which facilitated their identification with Islam. With what was known of their religion among the Makkans, Islam agreed without reservations. This included monotheism, transcendence of the Godhead, universalism, and a strict morality.

Judaism and Christianity were a different case. While Muslims considered some points of Christian and Jewish belief valid and hence agreeable, other parts were considered by Muslims to be foreign to the Semitic tradition and hence in opposition to Islam. The Qur'anic criticism of these religions belonged to the Makkan period of revelation when Muslims had little contact with any people of different faith except the Makkans. This criticism was hence independent of any Muslim sociopolitical involvement with Jews and Christians. Islam's criticism of Jews and Christians was severe, especially when it was felt they had tampered with their scripture, thus introducing human fabrication alongside genuine revelations, and when they were found to be deficient in the observance of the injunctions of their religions. Thus while Islam related itself to these religions as members of one family whose source is one and the same God, it also distinguished itself from what it regarded as their human distortions.

The Isra'-Mi'raj celebrates Islam's identity with Judaism and Christianity, represented in the story of the Prophet's night journey to Jerusalem, and by his reported discourse with the other prophets of God when he ascended to heaven on that night. While all Muslims believe that the Prophet did take the night journey and did ascend to heaven, they disagree on whether the journey and ascension took place bodily and thus constitute a miracle, or whether they took place in spirit and therefore constitute another instance of the same phenomenon of

The Dome of the Rock is a familiar landmark in Jerusalem.

communication between God and humans. What is important, however, is the question of why Jerusalem was chosen to be the locus of ascension rather than Makkah or any other locality. Couldn't heaven be reached from any place on earth? Evidently Jerusalem was chosen because that city was the religious capital of Judaism and Christianity, and the abode of the prophets, with which Islam sought to identify itself.

Tradition has preserved the details of the event as told by the Prophet. He was awakened at night by the angel who on many earlier occasions had brought the revelation to him. The angel brought to him a special steed which he mounted. The horse then flew through the air, enabling the Prophet to recognize the travelers on the road and their caravans. Once in Jerusalem, the Prophet tethered his steed to the "Wailing Wall" near a large rock. It is from this rock, famous throughout antiquity as a place associated with both Judaism and Christianity, that Muhammad ascended to heaven. The rock can still be seen inside the monumental building called the Dome of the Rock which has been constructed over it.

In Paradise, all the prophets assembled to meet Muhammad in prayer and praise to God. God instructed His Prophet to institute *salat* in Islam. Muhammad was taken on a tour of heaven and hell, Muslim reports of which have become the source for many romantic and speculative accounts of heaven in both Islam and the West.

In celebrating Isra'-Mi'raj, Muslims acknowledge the great unity of all the prophets and, consequently, of the religions associated with them. Abraham, Moses, and Jesus are accorded a very special place among the prophets as founders of the three main streams of the Semitic family of religions.

Chapter 4

The Muslim Family

The importance attached to marriage and family life in Islam is reflected in the many Islamic laws aimed at supporting and protecting the institution of the family. This chapter explores various aspects of the Muslim family: the role of the Muslim woman and the legal rights extended to her, the laws regulating marriage and divorce, and the benefits of the extended family.

WOMAN

Woman, in Islam, was created by God to be man's partner. The Creator built into both man and woman a mutual correspondence so that each would find contentment in the other. The Qur'an calls man and woman a "garment" for each other, signifying their reciprocal closeness to each other (what is physically and continuously closer to oneself than one's clothing?), their mutual interdependence. Although the Qur'an grants women the same rights as men, it allows that "the men have a degree above the women." As far as religious duties are concerned, however, Islam made the sexes absolutely equal. It has exempted women from these duties when they are menstruating, pregnant, or recovering from childbirth.

Unlike most other societies of the time, Islam, from its beginning, recognized women as autonomous legal personalities with civil rights. As a complete legal person the adult Muslim woman is granted title to keep her name forever. She has the right to acquire, keep, and sell property as she pleases in perfect freedom. Her consent must be obtained for any transaction involving her, be it the lease of her property, the cultivation of her field, or, above all, her marriage. She cannot be coerced into anything. Unless she is a minor, and hence dependent upon her parents or guardians, or unless she has appointed another person to be her attorney-at-law or representative, she must exercise her rights in person in order to make a transaction legally valid.

Woman, in Islam, is not considered the source of evil. In Islamic belief she did not tempt Adam; nor did the devil or death, whether physical or moral, come into the world through her. The Qur'an tells that God had prohibited Adam and Eve from touching a certain tree and that they disobeyed and had to be expelled from Paradise. It does not say that the act of disobedience was sexual; nor did it have anything to do with the "tree of knowledge." Islam regards sex as an innocent good and the pursuit of knowledge as a paramount duty, not as evil. Furthermore, the Qur'an adds that the disobedient act was repented and that God forgave its perpetrators. Evidently, the guilt was purely that of disobedience. The Qur'an even explains the act as the result of human forgetfulness (Qur'an 20:115) which Islam regards as punishable because of the tremendous importance it lays on moral responsibility. Hence, there is no "fall" in Islam, and no resultant "original sin" in any form.

Woman, therefore, is innocent. She is a positive good, a consoler, a source of happiness and fulfillment to man, as man is to her. For Muslims, sex is as natural as food and drink, growth and death. It is God created, God blessed, God instituted. It is not laden with guilt, but, like woman herself, is innocent. Indeed, sex is highly desirable. The Qur'an prohibits celibacy for the sake of God, and the Prophet ennobled marriage by making it his *sunnah,* or example, and hence the norm for every Muslim male and female. Like everything else pertinent to life on earth, Islam made sexual gratification of men and women a thing of piety, virtue, and felicity.

Since woman is not property or an object but a full legal personality, sexual intercourse cannot be a random affair but must be done with the woman's consent and with responsibility, a responsibility that falls on both parties. Sexual promiscuity is vehemently condemned because it is, by definition, a violation of responsibility of one or the other party. That is why Islam counsels its adherents: Have as much sex as you please, but always responsibly.

Male-female relations have to be ordered and governed if the ethical demand of responsibility is to be met. To this end, Islam provided a whole system of laws governing those relations, for it believes that man-woman affairs cannot be left to the whimsy of the moment nor to the arrangements of others. Marriage itself, as an institution, is re-

A Muslim woman of Isfahan, Iran. Although the dress of Muslim women varies from country to country, it is expected to conform to Islamic standards of modesty, no matter what the style.

garded by Islam as a solemn compliance with the ethical requisite of responsibility. In condemning sexual acts outside of marriage as punishable crimes, Islam does so not because sex is evil in itself but because it has been engaged in irresponsibly and out of passion.

Islam considers that in male-female relations there is a physical side and an emotional side, as well as a spiritual side. Further, it maintains that adultery is a fulfillment of the physical side, and that it is often entered into at the cost of the long-run emotional side, and always at the cost of the spiritual. For in adultery one partner is always using the other, or allowing himself or herself to be used, as an object. Where one partner has proper regard for the other, surely he or she should be willing to transform the relation into marriage. Marriage in Islam is not a sacrament but rather a civil contract by which the partners freely proclaim their plan to regard each other henceforth as ends, and not as means. Let us then turn to the laws of marriage.

MARRIAGE

Marriage in Islam is not a sacrament. It is a bond made not in heaven, but right here on earth. Like all human bonds, it can be dissolved. It is a pledge or contract by which the partners regulate their mutual relations. Like any other contract, it has a few necessary provisions. If these are satisfied, the contract may contain any other provisions the two partners agree to include. The contract requires that there must be two adults consenting in total freedom to marry each other. The minor may be given in marriage by his or her parents, but upon reaching adulthood—an age which may vary slightly from community to community, but which may not come before sexual maturity—he or she has the full right to consummate the marriage contract or to reject it. Even if the marriage had already been consummated, Islam gives the right to either partner, upon reaching adulthood, to dissolve it.

The second requirement is that the contract contain specification of two dowries, both to be paid by the male to the female. The first, which is to be given and received before consummation of the marriage, usually consists of gifts of jewelry and clothing which become the woman's personal property and hence cannot be taken from her without her consent. The second is a commitment that falls due only if the marriage is terminated by divorce. Since divorce in Islam is possible for the male by repudiation, the second dowry acts as the female's "insurance policy" against irresponsible conduct on the part of the male, and thus counterbalances the prerogative granted him by the law. If it seems to betray equality that the male alone may divorce by repudiation, this is more than offset by the deterrent power of the second dowry which a woman is free to specify in any terms and amounts she pleases and which may constitute the male's total economic and social ruin.

The third component of the Islamic marriage contract is the presence of two witnesses, one of whom must be a male, and their attestation to its contents or terms. The contract is not valid unless it is public, for when a commitment is made before one's peers, it is more likely to be kept.

Besides these three provisions the parties to the contract can add others as they wish, provided the additional provisions do not violate the law. A marriage contract may stipulate the style of life to which the man or woman is entitled. It can provide for the marriage to be monogamous by stipulating that it would terminate (and hence the second or deferred dowry would fall due) if the husband contracts another marriage. But it cannot stipulate that husband and wife shall cooperate in thievery, other crimes, or rebellion against the state.

Islam does permit divorce. As previously noted, a husband can divorce his wife by an act of solemn repudiation. But the law requires that such repudiation be made three times to be effective. After the first and second repudiations, the law demands that the husband and wife deal with their dispute and try to restore domestic harmony through marriage counseling and arbitration by near relatives or others of their mutual choice. On the third repudiation, divorce becomes final, though Muslims believe that God called it "most hateful." In order to prevent the husband from frivolously or irresponsibly entering into a divorce, Islam decrees that no man may take back in marriage a wife whom he had divorced unless that woman had married another man and had been divorced by him. Such marriage constitutes a terrible humiliation for both; and its specter acts as a second deterrent, after the second dowry.

A wife may divorce her husband by court decision, not by repudiation. In this case she would have to establish in court one of the legal reasons justifying divorce such as contagious sickness, prolonged absence, impotence, cruelty, adultery, lack of support, or the like. A divorce granted by the court is always final.

Islam also permits polygyny. That is, a man may have more than one wife (but not more than four) at the same time. Such polygynous marriages have never been the rule but the exception. Moreover, the law enables a woman to make her marriage monogamous, if she so wishes, by entitling her to write monogamy into her marriage contract. There are situations in human affairs where Muslims consider the best solution to be a polygynous arrangement. They feel that such arrangements may contribute to human happiness where there is an excess of women over men or where there are widowed or divorced women, often with children and devoid of support. The plural marriages of the Prophet in Madinah after the death of his first wife were of this kind. A refugee widow with five children whom nobody wanted, a divorced wife of a former slave whom everybody was too proud to approach, an old matron whose relatives the Prophet wanted to reconcile—such were the women he married in his later life.

Besides legal provisions, Islam prescribed a whole range of ethical directives concerning women. They are to be treated with love and kindness, for they are a gift from God. They are to keep their chastity, to run their homes, and, with their husbands, to implement the highest injunctions of Islamic society and state. Having declared women innocent, having invested men and women with identically the same religious duties and privileges, having recognized women as legal persons and endowed them with civil rights, and, finally, having protected women against the ravages of social chaos and license, Islam clearly afforded women greater honor and protection than most of the societies of the Prophet's time.

THE EXTENDED FAMILY

It is quite possible that some women may not be inclined toward married life as envisaged by Islam. Some women have a penchant for different kinds of careers—for art, science, or some productivity other than is usually associated with married home life. This need is not new. It did not start with the industrial revolution which extricated women from their homes to work in offices and factories. The need is as old as humanity, and has raised problems before women's careers took them outside their homes. However, the problem is more often than not that the career-bound woman wants to have both a career and marriage, home, and children, and finds the two options irreconcilable.

To relieve woman from having to have a career in order to provide for herself, Islam prescribed support for woman, whether minor or adult, by her nearest male relative on the same level as his own. This prescription is not suspended except when she marries, at which time her support falls upon her husband. When divorced or widowed, the prescription still holds. However, if she is divorced and is pregnant or nursing a child, her former husband is obliged by law to support her and her child for two years after childbirth. Since woman is this well provided for all the length of her life, Islam prescribed that she would inherit only half the share of her brother.

Nonetheless, there are women for whom even this economic guarantee is not sufficient. Some women are creative and their creativity may well demand external occupation for self-fulfillment. If a woman is the sole female adult living in a nuclear family, either her career or her home has to bear the cost. One of the two has to give in. Otherwise, she can have both only in succession—children and home in the early period of her married life and career in the later period. But advanced age and long absence from the period of learning might have already ruined her chances for a creative career. In this case, she would more likely be able to do supportive service as a secretary, assistant, sales clerk, or factory hand. If she were to take up her career in her prime age, the children would suffer, as would the happiness of the home. To fulfill themselves, humans need beauty, a measure of home leisure where beauty of ambiance combines with friendly converse and pleasant activity. This is not likely to be available in homes where both parents are out working. Such parents would not be prepared to give one another the quiescence each needs.

It would be otherwise if the home also contained other adult males and females, if it were an "extended family" home. Parents, sisters and brothers, grandparents, uncles and aunts, all living together, would give the home the care it needs so that the woman could pursue a career without feeling obliged or superfluous. For the home belongs equally to all. The love and attention the relatives give the children are a blessing because of the blood relation. This does not necessarily prevent the mother from putting her own touch to her quarters or to the home as a whole, nor from taking her children into her own care after work hours. The point is that in her absence, the house is not left unattended, or attended by foreign servants; and the children are not left to the television set, the foreign babysitter, or the day-care center.

Moreover, the variety of characters and personalities and of moods and temperaments in the extended family home provides the opportunity for everybody to do what he or she pleases in company of those who love one another most. Be his or her mood one of joy or despondency, of friendly converse or meditation, of hard work or rest, or an outdoor promenade or a private conversation, husband, wife, son, or daughter would nearly always find someone in the extended family to join him or her in that activity. If the mood is one of isolation and withdrawal, that too is permitted without offense or guilt, for the people in question are one's beloved, one's near relatives. Such company is absolutely essential for personal sanity and social health.

Humans need love, counsel, company, and altruistic concern as much as they need food and air. Total privacy can be obtained only at the cost of loneliness and is unworthy of it. The consequences of loneliness far outweigh the satisfaction which privacy sometimes furnishes.

Not only does the extended family make careers both within and outside the home possible, but it makes the whole of society healthier. The extended family is the best guarantee against psychic ills and aberrations of all sorts. Islam has not only recommended it as a good, but has buttressed it with laws. Every human in need, it prescribed, is entitled to the support of that person's nearest relative. In complement of this, it prescribed that a person's legal heirs are not only one's spouse and children, but all one's living parents and grandparents, and all one's grandchildren and their children. All these members of the family are hence kept together by love as well as by law.

Chapter 5

The Islamic View of Nature and Wealth

Muslims consider nature and wealth as gifts from God, entrusted to them for their enjoyment and use within the limits set by moral law. The Islamic attitudes governing the use of nature and the production of wealth are examined in this chapter.

WORKING WITH NATURE

It was noted earlier that people were created to be God's *khalifahs,* or vicegerents or managers on earth. This means that they are expected to interfere with the processes of nature so as to transform the world from what it is into what it ought to be. It was also noted that the will of God in nature is being fulfilled necessarily through the workings of natural law. Finally, it was pointed out that God declared everything in creation subservient to human beings, designed and/or redesignable to serve their happiness.

From this it follows that nature is not an enemy. It is not a demonic force challenging and inciting humanity to conquer and subdue it. Unlike the religions of antiquity, Islam has no myth or drama of creation. It does not hold the world to be a god, demigod, or giant fallen from favor. It rejects all such theories of origin and is hence free from any demonic powers to appease or subdue. Moreover, Islam does not regard the world as a fallen realm, doomed to alienation from God. Rather, Islam regards the whole of nature as profane (that is, other than sacred), an innocent creation which God created out of nothing for the enjoyment and use of humanity. Nature, Islam asserts, is a great, positive blessing, whose joys are advance payments on the rewards of Paradise. It is an orderly cosmos created by God as the theater where humanity is to do good deeds. Nature is perfectly fitted and equipped by the Creator according to the best measurement, the best form, the best pattern, and is hence absolutely free of any flaws.

In nature, happenings take place in accordance with natural laws, that is, with the will of God. Hence, it is orderly. But its orderliness depends upon its Creator whose will it follows. This will is not whimsical; the Qur'an describes it as eternal and immutable. Hence, causal determination in nature may well be trusted to function. This trust, which is the base of nature's orderliness, is a necessary requisite of humanity's vicegerency. For if humans are to perform in nature, the system would have to be trustworthy, that is, capable of producing given and predictable results. Otherwise, if human interference could not be trusted to produce the predicted results, then purposiveness is destroyed, and with it, the divine assignment of vicegerency.

Muslims have looked upon nature, following these principles, as an open book, a second revelation from God, which anybody who has cultivated the necessary knowledge and discipline could read. The Qur'an, they maintain, is easier to read. Its statement of the will of God is direct and eloquent. Nature, on the other hand, has to be "treated" to uncover her secret, her law, by scientific investigation and experimentation. But with some preparation, its truth is as public as that of the Qur'an.

This explains why the Arabs of the Arabian Peninsula, who have never developed any science to mention, fell upon the scientific legacy of classical antiquity with such enthusiasm. Around 700 C.E., people would travel from eastern Persia to Alexandria for a chemistry or botany manuscript and would gladly pay a thousand golden pieces for it. By 800 C.E., however, there remained little of the scientific and philosophical achievements of antiquity that was not well known and mastered by the Muslims. Gradually, it became clear that some of the presuppositions of Greek natural science conflicted with the Islamic notion of God.

The problem was not the concern of the scientists who continued with their work unconcerned with those deeper issues. The philosophers took up the problem and, in their hands, the vague assumptions were clarified and pushed to their ultimate conclusions. Cosmic order became determinism; matter became eternal; divine initiative and providence were denied. The Aristotelian categories were the seemingly irrefutable base. If natural law is truly law, its application must be universal. This leads to the conclusion that the world is a closed cosmos where nothing can happen except by a cause sufficient

*This irrigation project in the desert of Saudi Arabia
marks one way that Muslims have worked
to alter nature.*

to bring it about. But if such a cause is there, its effect must necessarily follow. Thus, the chain of causality envelops the world. God may have built up the system, but He does not run it. Like clockwork, it runs itself. Matter, the presupposition of everything, cannot be destroyed; it only changes form. Hence it cannot come into being; that is, it cannot be created. It is eternal, coeternal with God.

It was the great philosopher al Ghazzali who dealt the death blow to this kind of philosophy. Like David Hume who followed him almost a thousand years later, al Ghazzali analyzed the causal connection and found it implying no necessity. The observations of science may establish that an event called B will follow an event called A. But that does not mean or imply that event B is *caused* by event A. The judgment that A is the cause of B is only a generalization of probable validity, a validity which grows stronger the more often B is found to follow A, but it never reaches a perfect validity. If the scientist is absolutely certain that B will follow A, whence does his assurance come? It is his faith that the world order or state of being which has so far caused B to follow A will not fail to do so in the future. This faith is the product of religion, not science. It is the faith that God, who is the cause of everything in nature, is not a malicious God, intent upon deluding and misguiding His creatures, but a beneficent God Whose patterns in nature are knowable and trustworthy so that humans may efficiently fulfill that which ought to be.

Nature, we may conclude, is pliable and capable of change; and humans are capable of altering its forms to what ought to be. Agriculture, horticulture, engineering, and architecture—in short, civilization itself—have their basis precisely in such alteration. But no alteration performed out of vengence or resentment against nature, or without responsibility to the Creator of nature, can remain innocent for long. For if nature is not used as a gift from God given for moral purpose, its abuse is certain. If the moral purpose of God is denied, may nature not be abused? In Islam, no such abuse of nature is possible. For the secret working of nature is God's pattern and will, and the utility of nature is a divine gift meant solely for fulfillment of the moral law.

WEALTH

There is no limit in Islam to people's right to use nature except the limits imposed by the moral law. This law prohibits any use of nature that may hurt one's neighbor, which the universalism of Islam identifies with all people present and future. Within the limits of this requirement, people may draw from nature as much as they desire. This means that Islam favors a capitalistic system where the combined forces of nature, human labor, and accumulated science and wealth may be used to the fullest possible extent as long as no harm comes to others. Islam takes a definite stand against poverty, which it declares to be the work of the devil. People are responsible for their poverty, though when they suffer from poverty they are worthy of compassion and charity.

The Puritans believed that God's pleasure with a person is shown in the good fortune He grants to him or her. The Puritans had a deterministic view of life, of nature and salvation. They viewed God as the decision maker. When He chooses to be pleased with a person, He manipulates good material fortune to that person's advantage. Despite this divine predeterminism, Puritanism succeeded in inciting quite an economic revival in America. Anxious to appear blessed, that is, as a person with whom God is pleased, many Puritans overexerted themselves to become rich and succeeded in winning both wealth and, supposedly, divine blessing. For they believed in the Puritan doctrine. The more they prospered, the more their faith encouraged them to press harder; and the more they exerted themselves and produced, the more they succeeded. Muslims share this belief and strengthen it with the faith that people are obliged to remold nature and the world, if the meaning of their vicegerency is to be fulfilled. Muslims believe that God commands them to produce wealth, so that all may live and prosper. They thank God if their efforts succeed, and they bear it patiently if they fail. Muslims hold the decision of God and the result achieved on earth in inverse relation. If they succeed, and they must do so on their own, God will reward them further. If they fail, they have only themselves to blame, not God.

Every Muslim desires and plans to become a "millionaire" if he or she takes Islam seriously. Islam, however, warns that in amassing wealth, one should earn it. One should not cheat fellow humans of their wealth, but should produce one's own. Islam prohibits gambling because it is a game of chance and because its wealth, if it brings any, is not the result of effort and productive self-exertion. Such wealth constitutes no increase to the wealth of humankind. Islam urges people to produce *new* wealth, and holds the "self-made" person in special honor.

Islam is against the hoarding of wealth and has instituted *zakat* to discourage such hoarding. If consistently applied to a hoarded wealth, *zakat* would "eat it up" in one generation, the years needed for a tax of two and one-half percent to exhaust the stationary capital. Such wealth ought to be in production, invested in productive enterprises which increase the general wealth of humankind and provide jobs for more people. To ply wealth back into production is one of the beneficial effects of *zakat*.

To insure this continuing production of wealth and hence more employment and more production of real wealth, that is, of goods and services, Islam prohibits the charging of interest. Interest implies the accumulation of profit without taking risk, this being carried entirely by the borrower. In a sense, the lender too is commonly said to take a risk in lending the money. The fact is, however, that the lender's wealth usually increases despite a low rate of "bad debts." Otherwise no banker would stay in business for long. In addition, the lender's risk is minimized, since he or she exacts from the borrower all possible collateral and guarantees. Islam seeks to eliminate the class of financier by goading moneylenders to invest their wealth in production directly. Islam would certainly bless the effort of any group of people who form a cooperative credit society whose purpose is to store the savings of members and lend money to the needy among them *without interest*.

Once wealth is produced and appropriated, Islam requires that it be earned again, this time morally. It prescribes the *zakat,* or "sweetening," which, once paid to society, makes the wealth in question "sweet," now fully appropriable, investable, and/or expendable in any way the owner wishes. Islam also urges Muslims to give more, this time at no fixed rate or time and to anyone they wish to help. This form of charity is called *sadaqah*. Unlike *zakat,* it is voluntary and may legitimately be whimsical. By instituting it, Islam sought to give the wealthy the means of making their love-of-neighbor benevolence effective in their own immediate vicinity.

Islam rejects any practice that restricts the legitimate accumulation or distribution of wealth. For example, it does not subscribe to various methods of modern advertising—the false enticements to buy the products of industry and to create unnecessary needs for new products. Nor does it accept planned obsolescence as a way to keep the machines of industry running. Islam claims that other, more constructive ways must be found to increase the distribution of products.

In addition, Islam is against the imposition of customs, maintaining that a country that levies customs is inhibiting the free distribution of wealth around the globe and is encouraging a type of industry or agriculture for which it is not suited. A free worldwide distribution of wealth and goods, however, would not be effective without a free worldwide distribution of labor. Indeed, it would be Islam's desire to dispense with all customs and immigration institutions. Men and woman ought to be free to live and produce wealth wherever they wish without checks or hindrances.

Chapter 6

The Islamic World Order

By affirming the brotherhood of all peoples, Islam denies the concept of ethnocentrism and the doctrine of election. As a universal religion, it aspires to include all nations within the Islamic state. This chapter explores Islam's universalism, the comprehensive nature of the Islamic state, and the Muslims' vision of establishing a world order that encompasses all of humanity.

THE UNIVERSAL BROTHERHOOD
UNDER THE LAW

Perhaps the greatest implication of Islam's confession that there is no God but God (with its tacit assumption that everyone has been endowed by God with natural religion) is its universalism. All humans, in its view, are God's vicegerents on earth. All are subjects under moral obligation and all are objects of one another's moral action. Obviously, the greatest threat to this universalism, and hence to Islam, is particularism, the view that some people are to value their distinction from the rest of humankind more than their communion.

That humans do in fact differ from one another is a platitude. There are kinds of differences, however. Some are natural, like color, shape, height, and complexion. Others are natural but may be changed at will, such as weight, appearance, language, and many customs. Others, like intelligence, vision, smell, taste, and memory, may be cultivated but are less amenable to deliberate change. Undeniable as all these differences may be, the point Islam wishes to make is that they are irrelevant for measuring a person's worth, for planning and organizing one's societal activity and life. A human's creatureliness before God, the ultimate base uniting each person with all humanity, is far more important. To assert the opposite is to divide humankind into separate ethnic entities and to invite ethnic egocentrism, or nationalism, the view that denies advantages or privileges for the outsider to the benefit of the insider. Ethnocentrism can also be purely separatist and isolationist, by negating the relevance of the outsider to anything pertinent to the ethnic group, whether the outsider is dying of hunger and injustice, or overflowing with culture and prosperity.

That charity begins at home is not denied by Islam. Nor is this principle all there is to ethnocentrism. The latter, like all varieties of nationalism, asserts that the ethnic or national group constitutes the limits of goodness, of the obligation to all instituted bodies to bring about well-being and prosperity. Indeed, it even asserts the super-iority of the ethnic group above all others and tolerates, on the basis of that superiority, taking away from all others to give to its own group. From the Islamic point of view, this is condemnable aberration. Agreeing with the principle of priority to the next of kin, Islam insists on defining the benefits of society in terms of the well-being of *all* people.

Indeed, Islam recognizes in ethnocentrism something of a sinister nature. This is not so much the action of ethnocentrism, which can nearly always be justified on the basis of "charity begins at home," but the avowed base on which it rests its case: that the people within the ethnic group are "the master race," "people of God," "the chosen of God" while others are "the subject races," "people of the devil," "people of other inferior gods," or simply the creatures of the same God to whom they are related in a different way. This doctrine is sinister because of the deadening effect it has on the individual's awareness of his or her creatureliness before God which is shared with all human beings, and because of its stilling effect on an individual's will to act on behalf of humankind. It is also sinister because it believes that there is more than one God with two different creations, one superior to the other, or that one God created two creations so that one may have superiority over the other. The former view is polytheistic; the latter is contrary to God's justice and, ultimately, to His transcendence.

Islamic universalism holds that all people are entitled by nature to full membership of any human corporate body. For everyone is at once subject and object of the one and same moral law. The unity of God is inseparable from the unity of His will which is the moral law. Under this one law, Islam seeks to rally the whole of humankind on equal terms. It does not hold, or tolerate anyone to hold, a doctrine of election. Nobody, it asserts, has been predestined to any station. Such a view would contradict the moral nature of humans and the divine plan which is the purpose of creation, namely, that people—every person—may fulfill the moral law and achieve felicity. Nor does Islam approve of any "doctrine of the remnant" which affirms that although some or most of the members of an ethnic group may do wrong, go astray, or fall off from the state of election, there will always be a remnant that will not, and thus the ethnic group is justified to remain the elect that it claims to be.

This universalism of Islam does not preclude it from differentiating between people on the basis of their moral endeavor and achievement. Such preclusion would be equally contrary to the moral law which assigns "height" or "moral worth" in direct proportion to a person's moral accomplishment. Indeed, discrimination based on moral worth is not only well founded and tolerable, it is obligatory. This is what it means to honor the knowledgeable above the ignorant, the wise above the foolish, the virtuous above the vicious, the pious above the atheist or rebel, the just and loving above the unjust and hateful, and so on. Such discrimination has the positive quality of contributing to general moral felicity by enticing people to excel in the deed. To excel in the deed is the purpose of creation itself. It is all that matters.

THE ISLAMIC STATE AND A WORLD ORDER

Western political theory defines the state as consisting of four elements: territory, people with common features, government, and sovereignty. It cannot be without territory, and the territory must have boundaries. Its citizens must share some common features such as racial characteristics, language, customs, and history. Finally, the state must have corporate institutions and a government which together exercise sovereignty, that is, enforce in all aspects of life one will which is assumed to be the single will of the whole. This is a definition of the Western national state which is the creation of the last three or four centuries of Western history.

Such a Western state is radically different from the Islamic state. The latter does have a territory but this is not essential. It can exist without a territory, as well as with one devoid of definite boundaries. Indeed, Islam asserts that the territory of the Islamic state is the whole earth or, better, the whole cosmos since the possibility of space travel is not too remote. Part of the earth may be under direct rule of the Islamic state and the rest may yet have to be included; the Islamic state exists and functions regardless. Indeed, its territory is ever expansive. So is its citizenry, for its aim is to include all humankind. If the Islamic state is at any time restricted to a few of the world's population, it does not matter as long as it wills to comprehend humanity. Its citizenry need not be all Muslim and in fact has hardly ever been all Muslim. What is important is that the citizenry includes all those humans who agree to live under the auspices of the Islamic state because they approve of its order and policies. The Islamic state never binds people to its citizenship against their will. They are always free to move out, together with all their people, relatives, dependents, and everything they possess.

The Islamic state derives its constitution from the Covenant of Madinah which the Prophet granted to the city upon his emigration there in 622. The spirit of that covenant has determined every Islamic state in history. The covenant stated that the Muslims, regardless of their origins (they belonged to different tribes and nations), are one *ummah,* or community. That is to say, they constitute one corporate entity regulated by Islamic law. The *ummah* has its own institutions, courts of law, and schools for the education of its children. The *ummah's* governance with a view to self-realization—to achieving the full measure of its religion, its genius, its laws, its ethic and culture—is guaranteed. So is its perpetuity. For an *ummah* has the freedom to pass on to its offspring its legacy of religion and culture. The *ummah,* then, is a community living up to its own ideals, or at least seeking to do so in perfect freedom.

Besides recognizing and establishing the Muslims as an *ummah,* and hence wiping out their racial and tribal differences with the universalism of Islam, the Covenant of Madinah recognized and established the Jews as another *ummah,* on a par with the Muslim *ummah.* They too constitute a community that ought to be given full freedom to realize itself according to its own legacy and genius. It should have its religion, its social institutions, its own laws and courts to administer them, its own language and culture, its own ambiance and schools in which to bring up its children according to its own genius. It should enjoy all that is necessary to perpetuate itself.

In 630 C.E., or the year 8 of the Muslim calendar, the Christians of Arabia came to Madinah to negotiate their status with the Prophet. The Prophet received their delegation with open arms. He presented them with Islam and argued with them for three days while they enjoyed his hospitality as was customary with the Arabs. Some were convinced, became Muslims, and were immediately admitted into the brotherhood of believers as equals of all other Muslims. They became members of the Muslim *ummah.* The others were not convinced and remained Christians, but they did choose to enter the Islamic state as

The Prophet's Mosque in Madinah. In addition to being the place where Muhammad is buried, this mosque is the site of the mosque that was built by the Prophet himself.

3 THE 'ZAKAT'

One of the most important principles of Islam is that all things belong to God, and that wealth is therefore held by human beings in trust. The word *zakat* means both 'purification' and 'growth'. Our possessions are purified by setting aside a proportion for those in need, and, like the pruning of plants, this cutting back balances and encourages new growth.

Each Muslim calculates his or her own *zakat* individually. For most purposes this involves the payment each year of two and a half percent of one's capital.

ABOVE: *Zakat keeps the money flowing within a society. Cairo.*

OVERLEAF: *The first verses from the chapter 'Mary' in a Quranic manuscript written around 1400 in the style which prevailed in Persia and Iraq.*

A pious person may also give as much as he or she pleases as *sadaqa*, and does so preferably in secret. Although this word can be translated as 'voluntary charity' it has a wider meaning. The Prophet ﷺ said

'even meeting your brother with a cheerful face is charity.'

The Prophet ﷺ said: 'Charity is a necessity for every Muslim.' He was asked: 'What if a person has nothing?' The Prophet ﷺ replied: 'He should work with his own hands for his benefit and then give something out of such earnings in charity.' The Companions asked: 'What if he is not able to work?' The Prophet ﷺ said: 'He should help poor and needy persons.' The Companions further asked 'What if he cannot do even that?' The Prophet ﷺ said 'He should urge others to do good.' The Companions said 'What if he lacks that also?' The Prophet ﷺ said 'He should check himself from doing evil. That is also charity.'

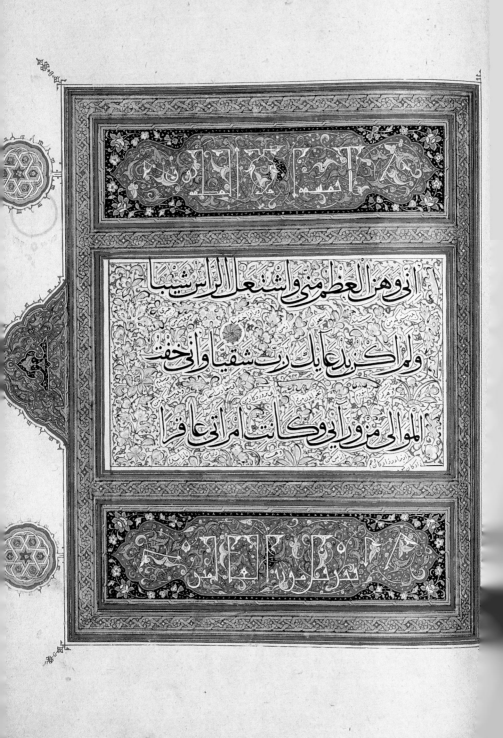

اِنِّی وَهَنَ الْعَظْمُ مِنِّی وَاشْتَعَلَ الرَّاْسُ شَیْبًا

وَلَمْ اَکُنْ بِدُعَایِٕکَ رَبِّ شَقِیًّا وَاِنِّی خِفْتُ

الْمَوَالِیَ مِنْ وَرَایِٔی وَکَانَتِ امْرَاَتِی عَاقِرًا

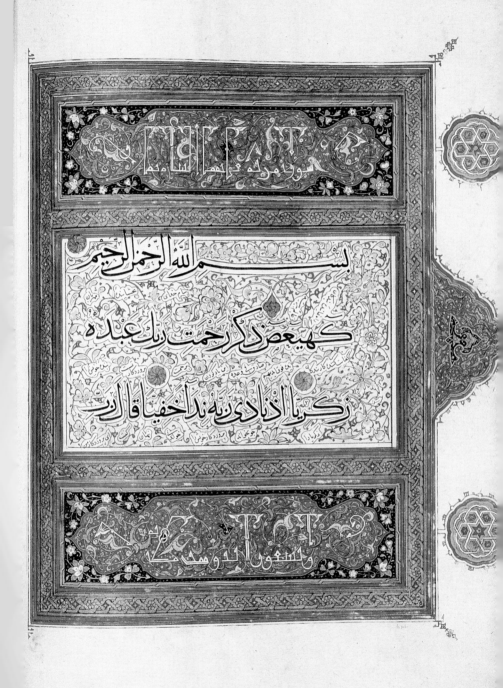

بسم الله الرحمن الرحيم

كهيعص ذكر رحمت ربك عبده

زكريا اذ نادى ربه نداء خفيا قال رب

Every year in the month of Ramadan, all Muslims fast from first light until sundown, abstaining from food, drink, and sexual relations. Those who are sick, elderly, or on a journey, and women who are pregnant or nursing are permitted to break the fast and make up an equal number of days later in the year. If they are physically unable to do this, they must feed a needy person for every day missed. Children begin to fast (and to observe the prayer) from puberty, although many start earlier.

Although the fast is most beneficial to the health, it is regarded principally as a method of self-purification. By cutting oneself off from worldly comforts, even for a short time, a fasting person gains true sympathy with those who go hungry as well as growth in one's spiritual life.

The annual pilgrimage to Makkah — the *Hajj* — is an obligation only for those who are physically and financially able to perform it. Nevertheless, about two million people go to Makkah each year from every corner of the globe providing a unique opportunity for those of different nations to meet one another. Although Makkah is always filled with visitors, the annual *Hajj* begins in the twelfth month of the Islamic year (which is lunar, not solar, so that *Hajj* and Ramadan fall sometimes in summer, sometimes in winter). Pilgrims wear special clothes: simple garments which strip away distinctions of class and culture, so that all stand equal before God.

citizens. Accordingly, they were granted the same status as the Jews and the Muslims. Henceforth they were to be an *ummah*, on a par with the rest, enjoying the privilege of living as Christians in fulfillment of their legacy of religion and culture and of their will to perpetuity. They did not live in Madinah, like the Jews, but far away, in lands separated from Madinah. Just the same, the Prophet included them, thus expanding the jurisdiction of the Islamic state, and sent with them one of his trusted companions to be his representative in their territory. From that moment on, their protection from foreign aggression as well as from internal subversion fell to the Islamic state. It was the guarantor of their freedom, of their Christianness, and of their self-continuation in history.

By the same logic, the Persian Zoroastrians and the Indian Hindus and Buddhists were included in the Islamic state as *ummahs* on a par with the other *ummahs* of Muslims, Jews, and Christians. The Islamic state was their guarantor and protector whose duty, as defined by its own constitution, was to enable each group to live in accordance with its own religion, ethic, and culture, and to perpetuate itself through the generations in perfect freedom. The Islamic state is thus not an exclusively Muslim state, but a federation of *ummahs* of different religions and cultures and traditions, committed to live harmoniously and in peace with one another.

Islam, however, is a missionary religion. How then is this federal system accepted as a way of life between Muslims and non-Muslims? Mission is certainly endemic to Islam. It flows from its essence as a universal religion. Every Muslim wishes that Islam would be the conscious religion of every person. In fact, Muslims believe that Islam was the original religion of every person but has been changed by time and culture into something else.

Islam also holds missionary zeal to be a duty incumbent upon every Muslim. This missionary spirit, or *da'wah* (literally, "calling" people to Islam), is not contradictory to the Islamic state. Indeed, mission is its ultimate objective. Therefore Muslims must carry out the mission both within and outside of the Islamic state. A verse of the Qur'an assigns the duty of converting the Arabs, the first *ummah*, to Muhammad. The first *ummah*, in turn, converted the other *ummahs* within the Islamic state. By logical extension, Muslims, including their Prophet, have understood the Islamic state to be assigned the same duty toward other states.

The principle which makes all this possible without contradicting anything that has been said so far is that of personal freedom. Under Islam, religious conviction is an entirely personal affair. Each person is free to convince and to be convinced. Unless and until one is convinced of the Islamic claim, one is perfectly entitled to be what one is and to continue to do so from generation to generation. The Muslims, therefore, may continue to missionize, but they cannot use force or subversion, which are punishable criminal violations in Islam. Both non-Muslims and Muslims are entitled to the full practice of their faith. But they are not entitled to pursue isolationism or to run their affairs, or the affairs of their *ummahs,* so as to interfere with each other's religious and cultural life. Either of these practices is based on ethnocentrism, or the superiority of one *ummah* over the other. Internally, the Islamic state cannot tolerate any encroachment of one *ummah* over another. Its duty is the same toward all: to keep the peace, to run the public services, to defend the totality, and to protect the rights and privileges of the persons and their *ummahs* which make up the state.

Externally, the Islamic state is ideological. It does have a world purpose which it pursues with all the power at its disposal. This purpose is the extension of itself to envelop the world. It approaches other states, tribes, nations, or groups with the proposal for them to enter an *ummah* within the Islamic state. Such entrance, it explains, does not mean the entry of a state's people into the Islamic religion, nor any diminution or change of any institution which has hitherto prevailed within it. Nor does it mean any alteration of its economic arrangement or the political sovereignty of its king, government, or governmental institutions. All these will remain absolutely the same and will be guaranteed and protected. Its entrance into the Islamic state means only that its relations with that state will henceforth be peaceful, that neither state will wage war against the other. It also means that a state entering the Islamic state will agree not to live in isolation from the rest of humanity.

The Islamic state is therefore not really a state but a world order, with a government, a court, a constitution, and an army. To enter it is to decide on peaceful intercourse with one's fellow humans and to renounce war between the *ummahs* once and for all. It would appear to the Muslim that not to enter it—to remain outside of it—is to assert the contrary and hence to mean either national isolation or war and aggression. That is why Muslim theorists have called the Islamic state "the House of Peace," a real world order. All that lies outside of it is called "the House of War." Entrusted to carry out this world plan, the Islamic state cannot rest until it succeeds in establishing this world order.

Force is not to be in the hands of any *ummah,* not even the Muslim *ummah.* It is to be in the hands of the Islamic state, or "world order," exclusively. It is to be used to put down rebellion with any *ummah* against its established institutions and authority; to restore to any *ummah* the rights, privileges, or properties which any other *ummah* might have violated; and finally, to defend the world order itself against its enemies. No other use of power is legitimate. Truly, then, the world order that Islam envisages is an ideal order of national and international relations, one which constitutes the only answer to the continuing malaise of the world situation. By comparison to it, a world peace based on atomic terror, on the balance of power, or on the imperial tyranny of any *ummah* over the others is considered by Muslims as satanic.

It may be asked, is it fair that the Islamic state, which draws its strength from all the *ummahs* within it, undertake the Islamic obligation of mission for Islam inside and/or outside its boundaries? The answer must take into account the following facts. First, the Islamic state is financed in times of peace with its collections of *zakat,* which is levied on all wealth of Muslims of sufficient means. No *zakat* is incumbent on non-Muslims. However, a *jizyah,* or poll tax, which is often one-tenth of the *zakat* or less, is collected from adult non-Muslim males, excluding all those who fill the ranks of clergy and public offices of their *ummah,* and then only if they are obviously capable of paying it.

Second, the army of the Islamic state is Muslim since the duty of *jihad,* or holy war (one undertaken to defend the faith of Islam), is a religious duty falling on Muslims alone. Others may join if they wish to, in which case they would be exempted from the *jizyah* and would be treated in exactly the same manner as Muslims. But they may not be conscripted by the government into military service. Their enlistment has to be voluntary.

Third, the Islamic state does not have to be a monolithic system where one and only one law, style of living, culture, religion, and world view prevail. This requirement has been relegated to the *ummah,* and it is the latter which acculturates, integrates, and assimilates all its members into the Islamic unit and preserves its Islamic existence.

These boys are studying the Qur'an in the New Mosque in Dakar, Senegal.

Non-Muslim *ummahs* render the same services to their non-Islamic members. That is why the Islamic state can afford to be liberal and pluralistic. In fact, its constitution is the only one which enables a state to be genuinely pluralistic, without attempt on its part to wipe out the differences between the *ummahs* under the pretext of "national integration" and "national unity."

The non-Muslim citizens of the Islamic state are free to opt for any religion, for any *ummah* within it. If they do not opt for an *ummah* within the Islamic state, they must emigrate, since there is no place for them within the Islamic state when their loyalty is to another state. But if they opt for an *ummah* within, they must conform to the rules by which that *ummah* lives and orders its affairs. A person may move from a non-Muslim *ummah* into the Muslim *ummah,* for such movement does not imply abandonment of the ideology of the Islamic state or the forsaking of loyalty to it. Movement from the Muslim *ummah* to another *ummah,* on the other hand, necessarily implies the repudiation of the Islamic state along with its ideology which comes from the religion of Islam. To convert out of Islam means clearly to abandon its world order which is the Islamic state. That is why Islamic law has treated people who have converted out of Islam as political traitors. No state can look upon political treason directed to it with indifference. It must deal with the traitors, when convicted after due process of law, either with banishment, life imprisonment, or capital punishment. The Islamic state is no exception to this. But Islamic political theory does allow converts from Islam to emigrate from the Islamic state provided they do so before proclaiming their conversion, for the state does not keep its citizens within its boundaries by force. But once their conversion is proclaimed, they must be dealt with as traitors to the state.

Fourth, and finally, it should be noted that the Islamic state is an Islamic idea, that it depends mostly upon the Muslim *ummah* for its manpower, energy, and mind. Furthermore, it is a unique phenomenon on earth. History knows of no parallel to it. If similar states were to be formed by non-Muslims, this would be a welcome development. For the Islamic state can then feel certain that the day will not be distant when it can merge with non-Islamic states since their constitutions would be similar. The need to form an all-encompassing "state" in which both the Islamic and non-Islamic states can deal with one another in freedom and peace would soon become evident to their citizens.

Chapter 7

Islamic Culture and History

The Islamic declaration that "there is no God but God" is magnificently expressed through the arabesque, a form of design that can be applied to music, literature, and philosophy, as well as to art, architecture, and calligraphy. This chapter considers the impact of the arabesque on Islamic culture and briefly traces the course of Islam from the time of Muhammad to the present.

THE ARABESQUE

It is clear from the preceding discussion that it is the task of the Muslim *ummah* to acculturate and Islamize its members and to preserve their Islamicity. The system within the *ummah* is quite monolithic, with built-in mechanisms for creative self-renewal and reform. Islam is a comprehensive way of life and is relevant for every aspect of life, for every deed. It is no wonder then that the *ummah* makes itself felt in all walks of personal and public (corporate) life. Islam seeks to put itself in evidence in the style of life at home, on the street, in the institutions, in the city—everywhere.

Islam teaches that God is indeed Lord and Master. Consciousness of Him is the first and last requisite. For to know Him as God—that is, as Creator, Lord and Master, as end of everything—is more than half the battle of existence and well-being. To know God as God is to love and honor Him; it is to lay oneself open to determination by His will. For only that is Islam, or submission. It is natural therefore that awareness of God is the objective of every endeavor, that Muslims surround themselves with all that reminds them of God, that everything within the *ummah* is God oriented.

Naturalism—the perception of ultimate reality in nature and the assumption that nature is its own norm and measure, that the good, the true, and the beautiful are in and of nature—is the antithesis of Islam. This is not to say that Islam is opposed to nature, but that it resists taking nature for God and thus reducing His transcendence. Nature is the strongest contender for the place of God. Its position has been ever rising in the consciousness of Western thought since the Renaissance which, in this sense, may be said to have dethroned God. Instead of God being the end and measure of all things, the Renaissance installed the human being as the crown of nature; for the human, it deemed, was the "measure unto all things."

These starting points gave the Western and Islamic cultures their respective sense of beauty. For the Western Christian affected by the Renaissance, the human being was the essence of beauty. The human body, soul, and mind were sublime. The Christian doctrine of incarnation, its idea of a God immanent in the flesh and hence in nature, was a departure from the Semitic notion of a transcendent God who is the absolute standard of beauty, truth, and morality, and led to the view that the human being is the absolute standard. Henceforth the whole Christian culture was to be transformed by this principle, just as Islamic culture remained true to the original Semitic vision that only God is God and, hence, that only God is the absolute norm, standard, and measure of all things.

Beginning with the Renaissance, Western artists began to paint, carve, and design in a way expressive of this naturalism. The church fathers, custodians of the Christian vision, were shocked at first, especially by the representation of naked bodies; but they quickly acquiesced to this invasion of Western consciousness by pagan and naturalist Greece and Rome. This invasion was pervasive not only in the visible arts, but equally in all other aspects of culture. However, the various areas of culture were not all invaded at the same time. One could argue that philosophy had to await the arrival of Descartes; literature, the arrival of Erasmus; music, that of Joseph Haydn.

The Muslims, on the other hand, developed the arabesque, a design applicable to decoration as well as to architecture, to painting as well as to calligraphy, to town planning as well as to literature, to horticulture as well as to philosophy. The arabesque design is built on the laws of nondevelopment, repetition, symmetry, and momentum. The first of these is a denial of nature whose law is certainly development, or movement through successive stages of growth ending in maturation, beyond which everything seems to be irrelevant to the natural process in question. Just as the Islamic view begins with a denial "no God but

These intricate, brightly colored designs decorate the ceiling of the Umawi Mosque in Damascus.

God," so does the universal pattern of Islamic art, language, thought, and style begin with the negation of nature as measure and norm, as embodiment, locus, or carrier of the sublime.

The second principle on which the arabesque is built is repetition and the third is symmetry. Nature is neither repetitious nor symmetrical. The leaves of the same tree may look alike, but each one is different from all the others. Likewise the case with symmetry. The arabesque denies naturalism through these two principles, but that is not their only function. They are the elements out of which the fourth principle of arabesque—that of momentum or motion from one repeated pattern to another, *ad infinitum*—is created. A row of bricks or a basket weave of threads or straws is both repetitious and symmetrical, but it has no momentum. The arabesque arranges the symmetrically repeated elements or patterns in such a way as to generate motion, to pull the spectator from one unit in the design to another, setting a course which, from the very nature of the design, can never come to a natural conclusion. The work of art itself—the tableau, the facade, the story, or the poem—does come to an end, as it must. But arabesque, or the design in it, never does. In graphic representation in a wall, a carpet, a miniature, or a panel of wood or masonry, the arabesque seems to continue beyond the natural limits of the object. The same is true of a composition of music or of poetry, where the elements and patterns differ, but not the design which never terminates when the performer or reciter stops, but creates a need to continue what has been experienced *ad infinitum*.

The purpose of developmental art is to arrest attention on the object developed, which is directly or indirectly a human state or condition. This is true even in the still life or landscape, which are given not for themselves but for the human character or personality standing, as it were, behind them. The nondevelopmental character of the arabesque aims at the opposite purpose. The arabesque does not arrest attention but, rather, keeps the pattern going in the imagination of the beholder. The momentum generated by the rhythm of the pattern carries the spectator outside the work of art and sets consciousness on an infinite march which will never end because it has no end. Here, an intuition is gained of the negative aspect of transcendent reality, namely, that it is infinite, is never given to human sense perception, can never be grasped immanently in nature, and hence can never be expressed. The arabesque does not express God but it does express sensibly and beautifully the inexpressibility of God.

It is therefore not by accident that Muslims surround themselves with objects of art which all tell the same theme: "There is no God but

God." The Muslim house, its facade, skyline, floor plans, interior and exterior decoration—all emphatically deny nature, saying, as it were, nothing in nature is God or even a vehicle for God. Where they have been invested with Islamic beauty and, hence, with arabesque designs generating a momentum toward infinity, their expressiveness becomes all the more eloquent. What the Muslim loves to hear, likewise, be it instrumental or vocal music, the chanting of the Qur'an or the recitation of poetry, embodies the same principles and expresses the same vision of the one transcendent God.

Calligraphy of the Arabic language is the supreme art of Islam. It is a double art. First, it is a visible arabesque. It consists of a malleable line which the calligrapher undulates, stretches, bends, inclines, renders in strait, broken, angular, or cursive design, decorates, and floriates into rosettes, geometrical or other patterns, making of the writing an arabesque as beautiful as any other decoration. Second, calligraphy has a discursive content. The words reproduced present something directly to the mind besides what is presented to sense. This is usually a verse from the Qur'an or a *hadith* of the Prophet. Making the word of God visible, beautifully visible, is the *raison d'etre* and ultimate purpose of the art. A verse of poetry, a proverb, or a common saying could also serve if its thought-content agrees with God's transcendence. In Arabic calligraphy, therefore, the discursive content and the sensory presentation enhance each other and thus make calligraphy the most popular and the most venerated art of Islam. Kings, princes, as well as commoners often lived their whole lives with a single wish—to produce, or cause to be produced, a copy of the Qur'an in beautiful calligraphy. Never before Islam, and nowhere else, did bookmaking ever become a genuine fine art.

This theory of aesthetics, grounded in the transcendent nature of God, necessitated that the mosque, the supreme public expression of Islam, be an empty building. Since Islam has no sacraments and no priesthood, the mosque had to be a place where worshippers stand singly or in rows to address themselves to God, without mediation. They did not need to surround themselves with any object. Presence of mind and a place to stand and prostrate themselves were all they needed.

The walls and ceilings of the mosque are covered with arabesques in marble, stucco, wood, or ceramic tile, denying mass, weight, opaqueness, and hence enclosure of space. Instead of enclosure, the mosque walls give the airy feeling of transparent screens of floating patterns which join the mosque to infinite space. The carpets, the pillars, the decorated panels, the crenellated skyline—everything expresses the same theme of infinity and transcendence with one voice. The bands, panels, and rosettes of Arabic calligraphy, reproducing verses from the Qur'an, repeat the same theme. Transcendence, or ultimate reality, namely Allah, touches every aspect of the Muslim's life. It pervades every product of Muslim culture and dominates every corner of the individual Muslim's consciousness.

THE COURSE OF ISLAM

Islam was born in Arabia. In a sense it had to be. Islam is the crystallization of ancient Mesopotamian (Semitic) religion and wisdom and it could only be reborn in Arabia for two reasons. First, Arabia was the only corner of the ancient world relatively untouched by the Egyptian, Greek, and Zoroastrian culture, and so the Mesopotamian legacy flourished there without adulteration.

Second, the Mesopotamian legacy in Arabia was assisted, bolstered, and preserved not so much in the religious practices of the pre-Islamic Arabs, but in their language and poetry. These were great preservatives. In them was fixed the Arabs' unconscious awareness of transcendence. Their language itself was an arabesque in its lexicography, syntax, grammar, and literary asethetics. Their poetry was the ultimate example of symmetry, repetition, nondevelopment, and momentum long before Islam. Nothing could have fitted the Islamic message better than the Arabic literary medium. There is perfect correspondence between them. Nowhere else was any such consciousness mirrored in any language. When Islam came, it built its whole case on the literary sublime character of its revelations—the medium which the Arabs (and only the Arabs) could readily and perfectly appreciate. They knew what is and what is not miraculous or sublime in that medium.

Before the death of Muhammad, the whole of Arabia had acknowledged the new crystallization of its innermost, even unconscious, wisdom. It saw in Islam what Islam proclaimed itself to be, namely, that it is the quintessence of all ancient Semitic history, of all previous revelations and prophecies; that it is the thesis of transcendence, of a reality which Arab consciousness recognized as alone ultimate and truly transcendent. Arabia stood poised, now that Islam revealed to Arab consciousness its identity and destiny as the message carrier of divine transcendence to the world.

Arabness, or this consciousness of transcendence mirrored in the Arabic language and poetry, had already penetrated to some degree the Fertile Crescent, Arabia's northern land bridge with Asia and Africa, before Islam. Indeed, the Fertile Crescent was Arabized in this sense by repeated migrations going back to Akkad in 3000 B.C.E. or earlier. The later influences of the invading Philistines and "men of the mountains," of Hittites, Egyptians, Greeks, and Persians, helped to confuse and veil that consciousness but not to destroy or fundamentally alter it. The Arabs held firm to all that had come to them from the pre-Islamic Fertile Crescent, whether it was language, works of art, law codes, or literature. No sooner had Islam presented itself to them than they acknowledged Islam as their own, not as something foreign but as something they had always known but were unable to express as clearly as the Qur'an had done.

The spring and summer of the Islamic Empire lasted five hundred years, from about 700 to 1200 C.E. At the beginning of this time the religion of Islam burst out of the desert and within a generation had created an empire that stretched from France to India.

The world of Islam was a great cultural and scientific center while Europe was still sunk in barbarism and ignorance. The oldest university in continuous use is the Al Azhar in Cairo, Egypt. In the Middle Ages it was the center of scientific inquiry. The Arabs introduced paper to Europe and invented the pointed arch without which Europeans could never have built their Gothic cathedrals. They sent apricots, rice, and sugar to Europe. Ibn Sina's *Canon of Medicine* and al Razi's *On Smallpox and Measles* were the standard textbooks of the medical profession for about eight hundred years. Ibn al Baytar wrote a medical textbook, *Simplicia,* that was still being printed in Europe almost a thousand years later.

Being avidly anxious to discover the will of God in nature, the Muslims quickly learned and assimilated the legacy of antiquity and moved far beyond it. Around 1000 C.E., al Biruni measured the earth's perimeter within inches of the most exact modern measurements and established the earth's rotation on its axis. Arabic numerals (1, 2, 3, etc.) replaced Roman ones (I, II, III, etc.). The Arabs introduced to Europe the Hindu idea of zero, or 0, and the idea of arranging numbers by units of tens and hundreds.

Cities sprang under the influence of Islam. They were the model of town planning, utility, cleanliness, and integration. Their colleges and schools, public libraries, public baths, recreation areas and gardens, running water and drainage systems were perhaps superior to many in modern cities. In Cordoba, Spain, one of the great Muslim centers, there was a complete system of night illumination. And all this occurred in the ninth and tenth centuries, when Europe's cities, the heirs of classical antiquity, could hardly boast of one paved street or of one public night-light other than the moon.

Muslim contributions to civilization are evident in the Arabic words which passed into the English language directly or through French, Spanish, and especially Latin. Following are a few examples from many fields: *albatross, gazelle, giraffe, popinjay* in zoology; *azimuth, nadir, zenith* in astronomy; *alfalfa, apricot, artichoke, coffee, cotton, lemon* in agriculture; *alcohol, alkali* in chemistry; *muslin, sash* in textiles; *candy, sherbet, syrup* in foods; *almanac, monsoon, sirocco* in meteorology; *algebra, cipher* in mathematics; *elixir* in drugs; *lute, timbal* in music; *alcove, minaret* in architecture; *caliber, magazine, tariff* in trade; *admiral, arsenal* in war and administration; *mattress, sofa* in furniture; *genie, kismet* in literature.

The Arabic language was, in Islam, the medium of revelation. It acted as the vehicle of transcendence. A knowledge of the language was necessary for the understanding of the Qur'an, the word of God. For the benefit of people who had not mastered the Arabic language as well as the people of the desert, grammars, lexicographic and etymological dictionaries, and syntactical analyses of all sorts were written by the thousands, as well as literary criticism and analysis of the Qur'an. In fact, every poem, common saying, or piece of oratory carried by memory was written down for the purpose of enabling the masses to master the language and understand the revelation. Everywhere the Qur'an was chanted in its original Arabic. Its verses decorated every room and house and punctuated every conversation and every treatise.

The religious vision of Islam was complete in the revelation, the Qur'an. That is why Islam does not have a religious history, that is, a history of its formation as a religion. Such "history" is limited to the biography of the Prophet, particularly the last twenty-two or so years of his life during which the revelation of the Qur'an was completed. The scripture was complete and its text canonized before the Prophet's demise despite the inexistence of an integrated written text, which came under 'Uthman in 646 C.E. It has remained the same throughout the centuries. Although the theologians wrote dissertations developing the creed, their enlarged texts were never the subject of legal implementation. Likewise, although Muslim spirituality developed a speculative dimension through mysticism, the pristine requirements of the faith as set out by the Qur'an and the Prophet never changed.

Animated by the vision the Prophet had imparted to them, his companions plunged themselves into implementing it and making it concrete in their daily life. The questions which preoccupied them were not speculative, but practical. What concerned them most was the method or means of realization. Thus they began the arduous tasks of translating the principles of Islam, as set forth in the Qur'an, into directives for human conduct, and of developing and establishing a viable methodology for such translation.

Many schools of juristic thinking developed in the course of time, five of which predominate to this day: the Hanafi school (by far the largest), the Shafi'i school, the Maliki school, the Hanbali school, and the Ja'fari school—all named after their founders and all coming from the second century after Muhammad. Judges and lawyers were educated in the thought of all schools; and wherever they traveled, from Spain to Java, they were honored for their knowledge and allowed to practice their art. The Shari'ah, or Islamic law developed by these early scholars, regulated the liturgy and the rites of birth and death, as well as the realms of personal status, procedure, contracts and torts, crime and punishment, and international relations. This body of law, which was largely responsible for the cohesion, stability, and uniformity of Muslim peoples throughout the centuries, represents a glorious achievement which to this day remains absolutely without parallel.

In the eleventh century, Muslim spirituality began to take a different turn. Prodded by an overenthusiastic love of God, as expressed in Arabic poetry by the famous mystical poetess Rabi'ah al 'Adawiyyah, converts from Gnostic Christianity and Judaism, from Hindu mysticism and Buddhism, began to interpret Islam in mystical terms, shifting its emphasis from the actual, where the divine will is to be concretized, to the spiritual. Psychic and introspective analysis took the place of legal and juristic study. Alchemy, astrology, and numerology slowly replaced chemistry, astronomy, and mathematics. Even the social health of the Islamic family gave way to the withdrawing, resigning surrender of the mystical brotherhood. Engagement in the affairs of society and state, so expressive of the Muslim's consciousness of vicegerency, was slowly abandoned for contemplative bliss and mystical experience. The Muslims became conservative out of the fear of the extinction of their faith. They withdrew from "history," from the "now," and became preoccupied with eternity and mysticism.

Over the years the caliphs, Muhammad's successors who were elected to lead the community of the faithful, began to lose their prestige and authority. They became the puppets of powerful army generals who squabbled among themselves and spread divisiveness generally throughout the empire. As a result, the state was left to whoever could grab it and keep it.

Thus the Islamic Empire became weak and internally divided, and was easy prey to an attack from the outside. Such an attack came in the thirteenth century with the invasion of the Mongols (Tartars) led by Genghis Khan. In his eager grasp the Muslim World fell like a ripe plum. One after another, its jewel cities were put to the torch and its people killed or reduced to bondage.

The Mongols conquered great areas of China, India, Russia, and Southwest Asia. In the latter, the tide was stopped at 'Ayn Jalud in Palestine by Ibn Taymiyyah, the first and greatest Muslim reformer. He managed to check the Mongol advance with an Egyptian army. In vain he tried to awaken the Muslims to their peril. The forces of mysticism consistently defeated him. Despite his military success at 'Ayn Jalud, he fell victim to the intrigues of the Sufis (mystics) and died in jail in Damascus.

Ibn Taymiyyah's hard work and death, however, were not in vain. He produced a whole library, over three hundred works, in which he diagnosed the Muslim disease in every aspect of life. The major villain was, of course, mysticism, which succeeded in reorienting the Muslims away from life, from the world, from reason and common sense, and delivered them to introspective meditation. Mysticism dulled the Muslim sense of realism and drew Muslims away from society, from their businesses, even from their families. Instead of pursuing the will of God as law, Sufism (mysticism) taught the Muslim to run after the dream of *union* with God in gnosis, or "mystical experience."

Even though Ibn Taymiyyah's ideas were not heeded, a miracle happened. In a generation or two, the Mongol hordes converted to Islam, the religion and culture of the very peoples they had vanquished. The conquerors settled *en masse* in Asia Minor and, a generation later, were ready to march again, this time under the banner of Islam. Still vibrant with the martial spirit with which they came from central Asia, the converted Mongols, now organized under the leadership of the house of 'Uthman (hence, the name "Ottoman"), pressed forward in the direction of Europe. The Byzantine and Russian empires crumbled at their advance. Vienna was besieged by them until the last quarter of the seventeenth century. The Black and Caspian seas became Muslim lakes. Between Vienna and Constantinople (renamed Islampul and later corrupted to Istanbul) they planted many Muslim communities and erected a new style of Islamic architecture on the foundations of the Byzantine.

The interior of the Blue Mosque, which was built in Istanbul in the early seventeenth century.

It was only in the eighteenth century that the Ottoman Empire began to decay from within for identically the same reasons which brought the downfall of their earlier Islamic Empire. It was also in the eighteenth century that the ideas of Ibn Taymiyyah revived, again mysteriously, in the very heart of Arabia, as yet untouched either by Ottoman decay or the West's ascendency. The reform movement was led by Muhammad ibn 'Abd al Wahhab. It hurled its fury against Sufism, calling itself *salafiyyah* (traditionalist) and seeking to reestablish the original vision of the fathers before that vision was corrupted by mysticism. Simultaneously or shortly afterward, similar movements swept over the entire Muslim World.

Practically all the reform movements in the Muslim World had to wage war simultaneously on two fronts: the internal front, where they had to fight lethargy, vested interest, and ignorance backed by the deposits of centuries; and an external front, imposed upon them by European colonialism. For the eighteenth and nineteenth centuries witnessed a merciless fragmentation of the Muslim World by the European powers and its subjection to the colonialist yoke, a process which continued through the first half of the twentieth century. The colonial powers were interested in keeping the Muslim World divided, weak, and undeveloped in order to exploit its human and natural resources and keep it as a market for their manufactured goods.

Today colonialism is at an end, but not its vestiges. Despite its pervasive influence, the Muslim peoples are racing the clock to catch up with the rest of the world. They have achieved great progress in the short period since they won their political independence following World War II. But their problem is essentially one of education, of making their citizens aware of their identity, their legacy of culture and civilization, and of developing their will to take their destiny into their own hands. Their record during the last three decades has seen many ups and downs. Some have flirted with Western ideologies such as nationalism, democracy, and socialism, with little or no success. But it was such Islamic activist organizations as the Muslim Brotherhood in the Arab World, the Jama'at-i-Islami in the Indian subcontinent, and the Muhammadiyah in the Malay Basin that fired the imagination and stirred up the will of the Muslim masses. Surely their Islam remains the strongest ideology Muslims ever knew. It is ready to move them again, if they but open their minds to its wisdom, their hearts to its appeal, and their arms to its energizing power.

Glossary

du'a'. Individual, private prayer to God which follows no prescribed form.

hadith. A report, handed down over generations, of the example of the Prophet's behavior which all Muslims should emulate.

hajj. The pilgrimage to Makkah (Mecca), the holy city of Islam in western Arabia.

hanifs. The upright, monotheistic, and moral people who were neither Christian, Jewish, nor pagan, and who upheld an idealized form of the Mesopotamian religious tradition.

haram. The area encompassing Makkah, the plain of Arafat, and other sites visited during *hajj*.

Hijrah. The emigration which refers to the escape of Muhammad from Makkah to Madinah, and marks the beginning of the Muslim calendar and the founding of the Islamic state.

'Id al Adha. The feast of sacrifice which ends the ritual of *hajj*, commemorating Abraham's sacrifice of his son Ishmael and indicating the Muslims' willingness to sacrifice for God.

'Id al Fitr. The feast which marks the end of the fast during Ramadan.

ihram. The garment worn during *hajj*, consisting of two pieces of unsewn white cloth.

imam. A leader who directs Muslims in worship and/or other activities.

Isra'-Mi'raj. The celebration which commemorates the Prophet's night journey to Jerusalem and ascension to heaven and which acknowledges that the Christian, Jewish, and Islamic religions have one and the same God as their source.

jihad. A war waged to defend Islam. Broadly, the obligation to spread the teachings of Islam and to combat injustice.

Jum'ah. The obligatory congregational *salat* on Friday.

Ka'bah. The small stone building in Makkah which Islam holds was first built by Abraham and his son Ishmael for worship of the one God.

khalifah. A vicegerent, or one who manages matters on earth by fulfilling the commands of God.

khutbah. The sermon delivered by the *imam* at the Friday congregational *salat*.

masjid. A Muslim house of worship. The word passed into the English language, with slight change, as *mosque*.

minaret. The tower on a mosque from which the call to worship is chanted.

muezzin. A person who chants the Muslim call to worship.

niyyah. The declaration of one's intention to perform a religious duty, for example, *salat* (worship), *hajj* (pilgrimage to Makkah).

Qur'an. The revelations which came to Muhammad from God and were collected in a book and canonized in 646 C.E. Muslims regard the Qur'an as the eternal word of God.

Ramadan. The ninth month of the Muslim year which is observed as sacred. During this month Muslims fast from dawn to sunset.

sadaqah. The Muslim institution of voluntary almsgiving.

salat. The ritual of Muslim worship.

sa'y. A ritual performed during *hajj* in which the pilgrims trot between two small hills seven times, signifying Hagar's search for water.

shahadah. The Muslim confession of faith in God and in the prophethood of Muhammad.

Shari'ah. The Islamic code of law, based on divine revelation, which regulates all aspects of Muslim life.

siyam. The fast observed by Muslims during the month of Ramadan.

Sufism. Mysticism as practiced by Muslims.

sunnah. An example of the Prophet Muhammad's behavior which is a standard of conduct to be emulated by all Muslims. As a collective term, all the reported traditions recording the Prophet's behavior.

tarawih. The special ritual of worship prescribed for the nights during the month of Ramadan.

ummah. Any group of people living within the Islamic state and under its protection, but which has its own religion and laws, its own institutions and customs—for example, the Muslims, the Jews, the Christians. Also the totality of the Islamic state.

zakat. The Muslim institution of wealth sharing which prescribes that two and one-half percent of one's total wealth be distributed to the needy.

Bibliography

Abdalati, Hammudah. *The Structure of the Family in Islam.* Indianapolis: American Trust Publications, 1976.

al Faruqi, Isma'il R., ed. *Historical Atlas of the Religions of the World.* New York: Macmillan Co., 1974.

Arberry, Arthur J. *Aspects of Islamic Civilization.* Ann Arbor, Mich.: University of Michigan Press, 1967.

Arnold, Thomas W. *The Preaching of Islam: A History of Propagation of the Muslim Faith.* New York: AMS Press (reprint of 1913 edition). First published in 1896. Also available in editions published by Kazi Publications and Orientalia.

Azzam, Abd-al-Rahman. *The Eternal Message of Muhammad.* Old Greenwich, Conn.: Devin-Adair, 1964.

Brockelmann, Carl. *History of the Islamic Peoples.* New York: G. P. Putnam's Sons, 1960.

Bucaille, Maurice. *The Qur'an and the Bible.* Indianapolis: American Trust Publications, 1978.

Gibb, H. A., and Kramers, J. H., eds. *Shorter Encyclopaedia of Islam.* Ithaca, N.Y.: Cornell University Press, 1953.

Grube, Ernst J. *The World of Islam.* New York: McGraw-Hill Book Co., 1967.

Haykal, Muhammad Husayn. *The Life of Muhammad.* Indianapolis: American Trust Publications, 1976.

Hitti, Philip K. *History of the Arabs.* 10th ed. New York: St. Martin's Press, 1970.

The Holy Qur'an. A. Yusuf 'Ali's translation (Indianapolis: American Trust Publications) is best. Also good are M. Marmaduke Pickthall's translation, *The Meaning of the Glorious Koran* (New York: New American Library [Mentor Books]), and Arthur Arberry's translation, *The Koran Interpreted* (New York: Macmillan Co., 1964).

Jamali, Mohammed F. *Letters on Islam: Written by a Father in Prison to His Son.* New York: Oxford University Press, 1965.

Kotb, Sayed. *Social Justice in Islam.* New York: Octagon Books, 1969 (reprint of 1953 edition).

Kuhnel, Ernst. *Islamic Art and Architecture.* Trans. by Katherine Watson. Ithaca, N.Y.: Cornell University Press, 1966.

Lewis, B., and Schacht, J., eds. *Encyclopedia of Islam.* 5 vols. Atlantic Highlands, N.J.: Humanities Press, 1960–.

Malcolm X. *The Autobiography of Malcolm X.* New York: Grove Press, 1965.

Nasr, Seyyed H. *Ideals and Realities of Islam.* Boston: Beacon Press, 1972.

Rahman, Fazlur. *Islam.* New York: Holt, Rinehart and Winston, 1967.

Sharif, M. Mohammed. *History of Muslim Philosophy.* 2 vols. New York: International Publications Service, 1963–1966.